IWCS Workshop: Language and Ontologies 2015

Held at the 11th International Conference on Computational Semantics (IWCS 2015)

London, United Kingdom
14 April 2015

ISBN: 978-1-5108-0228-5

Printed from e-media with permission by:

Curran Associates, Inc.
57 Morehouse Lane
Red Hook, NY 12571

Some format issues inherent in the e-media version may also appear in this print version.

Printed by Curran Associates, Inc. (2015)

For permission requests, please contact the Association for Computational Linguistics at the address below.

Association for Computational Linguistics
209 N. Eighth Street
Stroudsburg, Pennsylvania 18360

Phone: 1-570-476-8006
Fax: 1-570-476-0860

acl@aclweb.org

Additional copies of this publication are available from:

Curran Associates, Inc.
57 Morehouse Lane
Red Hook, NY 12571 USA
Phone: 845-758-0400
Fax: 845-758-2634
Email: curran@proceedings.com
Web: www.proceedings.com

TABLE OF CONTENTS

Extending OWL Ontologies by Cartesian Types to Represent N-ary Relations in Natural Language

Hans-Ulrich Krieger & Christian Willms
German Research Center for Artificial Intelligence (DFKI)
krieger@dfki.de | c.willms1@gmx.de

Abstract

Arbitrary n-ary relations ($n \geq 1$) can in principle be realized through binary relations obtained by a reification process that introduces new individuals to which the additional arguments are linked via accessor properties. Modern ontologies which employ standards such as RDF and OWL have mostly obeyed this restriction, but have struggled with it nevertheless. Additional arguments for representing, e.g., valid time, grading, uncertainty, negation, trust, sentiment, or additional verb roles (for ditransitive verbs and adjuncts) are often better modeled in relation and information extraction systems as direct arguments of the relation instance, instead of being hidden in deep structures. In order to address non-binary relations directly, ontologies must be extended by *Cartesian* types, ultimately leading to an extension of the standard entailment rules for RDFS and OWL. In order to support ontology construction, ontology editors such as Protégé have to be adapted as well.

1 Decription Logics, OWL, and RDF

Relations in description logics (DLs) are either unary (so-called *concepts* or *classes*) or binary (*roles* or *properties*) predicates (Baader et al., 2003). As the designers of OWL (Smith et al., 2004; Hitzler et al., 2012) decided to be compatible with already existing standards, such as RDF (Cyganiak et al., 2014) and RDFS (Brickley and Guha, 2014), as well as with the universal RDF data object, the *triple*,

subject predicate object

a unary relation such as $C(a)$ (class membership) becomes a binary relation via the RDF `type` predicate:

```
a rdf:type C
```

For very good reasons (mostly for decidability), DLs usually restrict themselves to decidable function-free two-variable subsets of first-order predicate logic. Nevertheless, people have argued for relations of more than two arguments, some of them still retaining decidability and coming up with a better memory footprint and a better complexity for the various inference tasks than their triple-based relatives (Krieger, 2012). This idea conservatively extends the standard *triple-based* model towards a more general *tuple-based* approach ($n + 1$ being the arity of the *predicate*):

subject predicate $object_1 \ldots object_n$

Using a standard relation-oriented notation, we often interchangeably write

$p(s, o_1, \ldots, o_n)$

Here is an example, dealing with *diachronic* relations (Sider, 2001), relation instances whose object values might change over time, but whose subject values coincide with each other. For example (quintuple representation),

```
peter marriedTo liz 1997 1999          peter marriedTo lisa 2000 2010
```

or (relation notation)

marriedTo(peter, liz, 1997, 1999) *marriedTo(peter, lisa, 2000, 2010)*

which we interpret as the (time-dependent) statement that *Peter* was married to *Liz* from 1997 until 1999 and to *Lisa* from 2000–2010.

In a triple-based setting, semantically representing the same information requires a lot more effort. There already exist several approaches to achieve this (Krieger, 2014), all coming up with at least one brand-new individual (introduced by a hidden existential quantification), acting as an *anchor* to which the object information (the range information of the relation) is bound through additional properties (a kind of *reification*). For instance, the so-called *N-ary relation encoding* (Hayes and Welty, 2006), a W3C best-practice recommendation, sticks to binary relations/triples and uses a *container* object to encode the range information (`ppt1` and `ppt2` being the new individuals):

```
peter marriedTo ppt1                           peter marriedTo ppt2
ppt1 rdf:type nary:PersonPlusTime              ppt2 rdf:type nary:PersonPlusTime
ppt1 nary:value liz                            ppt2 nary:value lisa
ppt1 nary:starts "1997"^^xsd:gYear             ppt2 nary:starts "2000"^^xsd:gYear
ppt1 nary:ends "1999"^^xsd:gYear               ppt2 nary:ends "2010"^^xsd:gYear
```

As we see from this small example, a quintuple is represented by five triples. The relation name is retained, however, the range of the relation changes from, say, `Person` to the type of the container object which we call here `PersonPlusTime`.

Rewriting ontologies to the *latter* representation is clearly time consuming, as it requires further classes, redefines property signatures, and rewrites relation instances, as shown by the *marriedTo* example. In addition, reasoning and querying with such representations is extremely complex, expensive, and error-prone. Unfortunately, the *former* tuple-based representation which argues for additional (temporal) arguments is *not* supported by ontology editors today, as it would require to deal with general relations.

2 What this Paper is (Not) About & Related Approaches

We would like to make clear that this paper is *not* about developing a theory for yet another new DL which permits n-ary relations. The approach presented here suggests that the concepts of *domain* and *range* of a relation are still useful when extending a binary relation with more arguments, instead of talking about the *arity* of a relation in general. We furthermore suggest in Section 6 to introduce so-called *extra arguments* which neither belong to the domain nor the range of a relation, and can be seen, as well, should be used as a kind of relation instance annotation. In the course of the paper, we also indicate that most of the entailment rules for RDFS (Hayes, 2004) and OWL Horst/OWL 2 RL (ter Horst, 2005; Motik et al., 2012) can be extended by Cartesian types and n-ary relations, and present an incomplete set of rules in Figure 1. Our approach takes a liberal stance in that it neither ask for the "nature" or "use" of the arguments (e.g., whether they are time points), nor for a (sound, complete, terminating, ...) set of tableau or entailment rules. In fact, if we would take this into account, we would end up in a potentially infinite number of different sets of rules, some of them requiring additional (lightweight) tests and actions, going beyond simple symbol matching; see (Krieger, 2012) for such a set of rules that model valid time, turning binary relations into quaternary ones. For various reasons, we propose a general restriction on the use of Cartesian types in Section 5, viz., to avoid typing individuals with Cartesian types and to maintain still singleton typing. The practical accomplishment of this paper lies in an extension of the Protégé editor for Cartesian types and n-ary relations that should be complemented by application-independent, but also domain-specific rules for a given application domain (e.g., to address *valid time*).

Since the early days of KL-ONE, DLs supporting relations with more than two arguments have been discussed, e.g., NARY[KANDOR] (Schmolze, 1989), $\mathcal{CIFR}$ (De Giacomo and Lenzerini, 1994), $\mathcal{DLR}$ (Calvanese et al., 1997), or $\mathcal{GF}1^-$ (Lutz et al., 1999). Especially Schmolze (1989) argued that "the advantages for allowing *direct* representation of n-ary relations far outweigh the reasons for the restriction" (i.e., restricting $n \leq 2$). To the best of our knowledge and with the exception of NARY[KANDOR], these DL languages have still remained theoretical work. In (Krieger, 2013), we presented an implemented theory-agnostic forward chainer, called *HFC*, which is comparable to popular semantic repositories such as Jena or OWLIM and which supports arbitrary n-tuples. The engine is able to run non-builtin entailment rule sets à la OWL Horst/OWL 2 RL and comes with a conservative extension of these OWL dialects for *valid time* (Krieger, 2012). Further rule regimes are possible as long as they are expressible in *HFC*'s rule language which permits standard symbol matching, additional LHS tests, and RHS actions.

3 Extending Ontologies through Cartesian Types

Modern ontologies make use of standards, defined and coordinated by the W3C, such as XSD, RDF, RDFS, or OWL. OWL, as an instance of the description logic family, describes a domain in terms of classes (concepts), binary properties (roles), and instances (individuals). Complex expressions, so-called *axioms*, are defined via concept-forming operators (viz., subsumption and equivalence). The entirety of all such axioms which can be separated into those dealing with terminological knowledge (TBox), relational knowledge (RBox), and assertional knowledge (ABox), is usually called an *ontology* today.

Ontology editors which are geared towards RDF and OWL are thus *not* able to define n-ary relations *directly* in the RBox, nor are they capable of stating arbitrary tuples (instances of n-ary relations) in the ABox (together with Cartesian types in the TBox; see below). This would require an extension of the triple data model, or equivalently, allowing for n-ary relations ($n > 2$).

Formally, the extension of a binary relation p, can be seen as a (potentially infinite) set of pairs (s, o), coming from the Cartesian product of its *domain* $\mathbb{D}$ and *range* $\mathbb{R}$: $p \subseteq \mathbb{D} \times \mathbb{R}$. We then often say that a relation p is *defined* on $\mathbb{D}$, say, the *marriedTo* relation is *defined* on *Person*.

Now, in order to allow for more than two arguments, we decompose $\mathbb{R}$, leading to $p \subseteq \mathbb{D} \times \mathbb{R}_1 \times \cdots \times \mathbb{R}_n$. Note that we still make a distinction between domain $\mathbb{D}$ and range $\mathbb{R} = \mathbb{R}_1 \times \cdots \times \mathbb{R}_n$, and still say that p is *defined* on $\mathbb{D}$. Coming back to the previous section and the quaternary *marriedTo* relation, we can say that

$$\textit{marriedTo} \subseteq \textit{Person} \times \textit{Person} \times \textit{Year} \times \textit{Year}$$

For reasons that will become clear in a moment, not only the range but also the domain of a relation can, in principle, be deconstructed: $p \subseteq (\mathbb{D}_1 \times \cdots \times \mathbb{D}_m) \times (\mathbb{R}_1 \times \cdots \times \mathbb{R}_n)$. When it is clear from the context, we often omit the parentheses and simply write $p \subseteq \mathbb{D}_1 \times \cdots \times \mathbb{D}_m \times \mathbb{R}_1 \times \cdots \times \mathbb{R}_n$. We then say that the domain of p is $\mathbb{D}_1 \times \cdots \mathbb{D}_m$ and the range is $\mathbb{R}_1 \times \cdots \times \mathbb{R}_n$, thus p becomes an $(m + n)$-ary relation. Again, we say that p is defined on $\mathbb{D}_1 \times \cdots \mathbb{D}_m$.

Graphically, such an extension is easy write down. Let us start, again, with binary relations and let us picture the resulting graph for the following set $\{p(a, b), q(b, c), q(b, d), r(b, e)\}$ of binary relation instances by using directed labeled edges:

$$\begin{array}{ccccc} & & & & c \\ & & & {}^{q}\nearrow & \\ a & \xrightarrow{p} & b & \xrightarrow{q} & d \\ & & & {}^{r}\searrow & \\ & & & & e \end{array}$$

Ontology editors such as Protégé (Horridge, 2004) essentially use such a representation: properties are defined on certain classes and ontology or ABox) population reduces to filling missing range arguments for specific instances.

But how do we depict the following set of relation instances

$$\{r((a, b, c), (d)), p((a, b, c), (a, x)), q((a, x), (y, z)\}$$

of arity 4 and 5, resp? Quite easy, simply by replacing individuals (= singles) in domain and range position through general tuples:

$$(d) \xleftarrow{r} (a, b, c) \xrightarrow{p} (a, x) \xrightarrow{q} (y, z)$$

The "problem" with this kind of graph representation is that we are still using a kind of container (denoted by the parentheses) which groups both domain elements $\mathbb{D}_i$ ($1 \leq i \leq m$) and range elements $\mathbb{R}_j$ ($1 \leq j \leq n$). But this is something we want to avoid as explicated before (recall the *N-ary relation encoding* example from Section 1).

The answer to all this is already laying before us and has already been introduced, viz., *Cartesian* types (remember the $\times_i \mathbb{D}_i$ and $\times_j \mathbb{R}_j$ notation). This, however, will require to extend the descriptive expressiveness of the TBox, RBox, and ABox of an ontology.

4 Cartesian Types in TBox, RBox, and ABox

Protégé (and other ontology editors such as TopBraid) displays the *class subsumption hierarchy* using *indentation*, e.g.,

```
▽ Entity
  ▽ Object
    ▽ Agent
      ▷ Group
      ▽ Person
        ▷ Man
        ▷ Woman
```

These concepts can be seen as *singles* (or singletons), representing a Cartesian product of only one element. Thus the class `Person` can be seen as the tuple `(Person)`, consisting of one tuple element. Similarly, when considering the *marriedTo* relation, we might view the range type as the Cartesian type `(Person,Year,Year)`. Clearly, neither does `(Person)` subsume `(Person,Year,Year)`, nor does the opposite case hold—they are incompatible, for which we write

$$(\texttt{Person}) \bowtie (\texttt{Person}, \texttt{Year}, \texttt{Year})$$

However, the following subsumption relations do hold, given the above type hierarchy:

$$(\texttt{Man}, \texttt{Year}, \texttt{Year}) \sqsubseteq (\texttt{Person}, \texttt{Year}, \texttt{Year})$$
$$(\texttt{Woman}, \texttt{Year}, \texttt{Year}) \sqsubseteq (\texttt{Person}, \texttt{Year}, \texttt{Year})$$
$$(\texttt{Person}, \texttt{Year}, \texttt{Year}) \sqsubseteq (\texttt{Agent}, \texttt{Year}, \texttt{Year})$$
$$(\texttt{Group}, \texttt{Year}, \texttt{Year}) \sqsubseteq (\texttt{Agent}, \texttt{Year}, \texttt{Year})$$

Now let $\mathcal{C}$ denote the set of concepts, $\mathcal{R}$ denote the set of all relations, and $\mathcal{I}$ denote the set of all instances. Quite naturally, the subsumption relation for concepts $\sqsubseteq \subseteq \mathcal{C} \times \mathcal{C}$ can be easily extended to Cartesian types:

$$\times_{i=1}^{m} C_i \sqsubseteq \times_{j=1}^{n} D_i \text{ **iff** } m = n \text{ **and** } C_i \sqsubseteq D_i, \text{ **for all** } i \in \{1, \ldots, m\}$$

Given such an extension, many of the standard entailment rules from (Hayes, 2004) and (ter Horst, 2005) can be easily adjusted, but also two new rules, called (ctsub) and (ctequiv), need to be introduced which propagate Cartesian type subsumption and equivalence down to their component classes (see Figure 1 for a representative, non-complete set of extended rules).

5 A Restriction on the Use of Cartesian Types

The extension introduced so far would even allow us to type *individuals* $a \in \mathcal{I}$ with any Cartesian type $\times_{i=1}^{m} C_i$ $(m \geq 1)$ for which we might then write $\times_{i=1}^{m} C_i(a)$. This would make it possible to naturally extend, e.g., the universal instantiation schema (rdfs9) from Hayes (2004) with Cartesian types, viz.,

$$\text{(rdfs9)} \quad \times_{i=1}^{m} C_i(a) \wedge \times_{i=1}^{m} C_i \sqsubseteq \times_{i=1}^{m} D_i \rightarrow \times_{i=1}^{m} D_i(a)$$

Such an extension is attractive, but has severe drawbacks. It makes domain and range inference more complex and would require a stronger descriptive apparatus, as it will become necessary to group and access *parts* of the domain and/or range arguments in order to indicate the true number of arguments of a relation, but also to indicate the proper argument types. This would become important when checking relation instances against their relation signature.

Consider, for instance, a quaternary relation $p \subseteq \mathbb{D} \times \mathbb{R}_1 \times \mathbb{R}_2 \times \mathbb{R}_3$ that seems to come with three *range* arguments. However, by typing individuals with Cartesian types, the above relation can be binary, ternary (two possibilities), or quaternary, depending on how we interpret the range arguments:

- $p \subseteq \mathbb{D} \times (\mathbb{R}_1 \times \mathbb{R}_2 \times \mathbb{R}_3)$
- $p \subseteq \mathbb{D} \times (\mathbb{R}_1 \times \mathbb{R}_2) \times \mathbb{R}_3$
- $p \subseteq \mathbb{D} \times \mathbb{R}_1 \times \mathbb{R}_2 \times \mathbb{R}_3$
- $p \subseteq \mathbb{D} \times \mathbb{R}_1 \times (\mathbb{R}_2 \times \mathbb{R}_3)$

And there are even further complex embeddings possible (remember type theory), such as

- $p \subseteq \mathbb{D} \times (\mathbb{R}_1 \times (\mathbb{R}_2 \times \mathbb{R}_3))$
- $p \subseteq \mathbb{D} \times ((\mathbb{R}_1 \times \mathbb{R}_2) \times \mathbb{R}_3)$

(ctsub) $\times_{i=1}^{m} C_i \sqsubseteq \times_{i=1}^{m} D_i \rightarrow \bigwedge_{i=1}^{m} C_i \sqsubseteq D_i$

(rdfs11) $\times_{i=1}^{m} C_i \sqsubseteq \times_{i=1}^{m} D_i \wedge \times_{i=1}^{m} D_i \sqsubseteq \times_{i=1}^{m} E_i \rightarrow \times_{i=1}^{m} C_i \sqsubseteq \times_{i=1}^{m} E_i$

(ctequiv) $\times_{i=1}^{m} C_i \equiv \times_{i=1}^{m} D_i \rightarrow \bigwedge_{i=1}^{m} C_i \equiv D_i$

(rdfp12c) $\times_{i=1}^{m} C_i \sqsubseteq \times_{i=1}^{m} D_i \wedge \times_{i=1}^{m} D_i \sqsubseteq \times_{i=1}^{m} C_i \rightarrow \times_{i=1}^{m} C_i \equiv \times_{i=1}^{m} D_i$

(rdfs2) $\forall P^{-}.\ \times_{i=1}^{m} C_i \wedge P(\times_{i=1}^{m} a_i, \times_{j=1}^{n} b_j) \rightarrow \bigwedge_{i=1}^{m} C_i(a_i)$

(rdfs3) $\forall P.\ \times_{j=1}^{n} D_j \wedge P(\times_{i=1}^{m} a_i, \times_{j=1}^{n} b_j) \rightarrow \bigwedge_{j=1}^{n} D_j(b_j)$

(rdfs7x) $P \sqsubseteq Q \wedge P(\times_{i=1}^{m} a_i, \times_{j=1}^{n} b_j) \rightarrow Q(\times_{i=1}^{m} a_i, \times_{j=1}^{n} b_j)$

(rdfp1) $\leq 1P \wedge P(\times_{i=1}^{m} a_i, \times_{j=1}^{n} b_j) \wedge P(\times_{i=1}^{m} a_i, \times_{j=1}^{n} c_j) \rightarrow \bigwedge_{j=1}^{n} \{b_j\} \equiv \{c_j\}$

(rdfp3) $P \equiv P^{-} \wedge P(\times_{i=1}^{m} a_i, \times_{i=1}^{m} b_i) \rightarrow P(\times_{i=1}^{m} b_i, \times_{i=1}^{m} a_i)$

(rdfp4) $P^{+} \sqsubseteq P \wedge P(\times_{i=1}^{m} a_i, \times_{i=1}^{m} b_i) \wedge P(\times_{i=1}^{m} b_i, \times_{i=1}^{m} c_i) \wedge \rightarrow P(\times_{i=1}^{m} a_i, \times_{i=1}^{m} c_i)$

Figure 1: Entailment rules using Cartesian types ($C_i, D_j, E_k \in \mathcal{C}$; $P, Q \in \mathcal{R}$; $a., b., c. \in \mathcal{I}$). Note that the notation $P(\times_{i=1}^{m} a_i, \times_{j=1}^{n} b_j)$ in the above rules does *not* indicate that P is a binary relation, but instead is of arity $m + n$ *and* $a_1, \ldots, a_m$ are the domain and $b_1, \ldots, b_n$ the range arguments for this specific relation instance of P. The names for the extended rule schemata are taken from (Hayes, 2004) and (ter Horst, 2005). (ctsub) and (ctequiv) are brand-new entailment rules for Cartesian types. The correctness of (rdfp4), addressing the transitivity of P, depends on the interpretation of the application domain (for instance, whether certain arguments are employed for expressing the validity of a fluent (the atemporal fact) over time; see also Section 6).

Mainly for this reason, we enforce that atomic *individuals* from $\mathcal{I}$ can only be typed to *single* concepts (singletons), and thus the relation signature

$$p \subseteq \mathbb{D}_1 \times \cdots \times \mathbb{D}_m \times \mathbb{R}_1 \times \cdots \times \mathbb{R}_n$$

is intended to mean that p takes *exactly* m domain arguments and *exactly* n range arguments, such that $\mathbb{D}_1, \ldots, \mathbb{D}_m, \mathbb{R}_1, \ldots, \mathbb{R}_n \in \mathcal{C}$ must be the case.

6 Extra Arguments

This section deals with what we call *extra arguments*, arguments that neither belong to the domain nor the range of an $(m + n)$-ary relation, but can be seen as a kind of additional *annotation*, belonging to specific relation instances.[1]

Let us start with a binary relation ($m, n = 1$) and consider, again, the non-temporal version of *marriedTo* which is a true *symmetric* relation, expressed by the following instantiated entailment rule:

$$\mathit{marriedTo}(i, j) \rightarrow \mathit{marriedTo}(j, i)$$

Now, if we add time (b = begin; e = end), it becomes a quaternary relation as indicated before (for better readability, we separate the domain and range arguments from one another by using parentheses):

$$\checkmark\ \mathit{marriedTo}(i, (j, b, e)) \rightarrow \mathit{marriedTo}(j, (i, b, e))$$

In this sense, the temporal interval $[b, e]$ specifies the valid time in which the fluent (the atemporal statement) *marriedTo*(i, j) is true. By applying the extended rule (rdfp3) from Figure 1 for symmetry, we see that something clearly goes wrong:

$$\lightning\ \mathit{marriedTo}(i, (j, b, e)) \rightarrow \mathit{marriedTo}((j, b, e), i)$$

[1] This is like having annotation properties for *relation instances*, but OWL unfortunately offers this service only for classes, properties, and individuals.

as symmetric relations assume the same number of arguments in domain and range position! Our example above thus needs to be modified. One solution would be to reduplicate the starting and ending points, so we would end up in a sexternary relation:

$$\textit{marriedTo}((i, \underline{b, e}), (j, \underline{b, e})) \rightarrow \textit{marriedTo}((j, \underline{b, e}), (i, \underline{b, e}))$$

This is *not* an appealing solution as the structures become larger, and rules and queries are harder to formulate, read, debug, and process. We thus like to extend relations $p \subseteq \mathbb{D}_1 \times \cdots \times \mathbb{D}_m \times \mathbb{R}_1 \times \cdots \times \mathbb{R}_n$ by further arguments $\mathbb{A}_1 \times \cdots \times \mathbb{A}_o$, so that p becomes

$$p \subseteq \mathbb{D}_1 \times \cdots \times \mathbb{D}_m \times \mathbb{R}_1 \times \cdots \times \mathbb{R}_n \times \mathbb{A}_1 \times \cdots \times \mathbb{A}_o$$

or simply write $p \subseteq \mathbb{D} \times \mathbb{R} \times \mathbb{A}$. For the *marriedTo* example, we might choose Person from the ontology above and the XSD type gYear: $\mathbb{D}$ = Person, $\mathbb{R}$ = Person, $\mathbb{A}$ = gYear $\times$ gYear.

Thus by having these *extra* arguments, we can keep the entailment rules from Figure 1, extended, of course, by the additional annotations.[2] Besides having extra arguments for *valid time*, other areas are conceivable here, viz., *transaction time, space, sentiment, uncertainty, negation, vagueness, or graded information*.

7 Extensions to Protégé

In order to make Cartesian types available in Protégé, we will extend the *OWL Classes*, *Properties*, and *Individuals* tabs.

TBox: *OWL Classes* Tab

- *subclass explorer* pane (left column)
  extension of the subclass hierarchy towards Cartesian types.
- *class editor* pane (right column)
  depicting the right properties defined on a Cartesian type (domain); depicting the right Cartesian range types for the defined properties.

RBox: *Properties* Tab

- *property browser* pane (left column)
  extension of the property hierarchy towards Cartesian types.
- *property editor* pane (right column)
  extension of the domain and range boxes towards Cartesian types.
- **new:** *extra arguments* (part of the *property editor* pane)
  further definition box for the extra arguments.

ABox: *Individuals* Tab

- *class browser* pane (left column)
  extension of the subclass hierarchy towards Cartesian types.
- *instance browser* pane (middle column)
  possibility to generate sequence instances defined on Cartesian types (= sequences of instances of singleton types).
- *property editor* pane (right column)
  depicting the right properties defined on a sequence instance; allowing to choose or construct the range arguments; allowing to choose or construct the extra arguments.

Not only the graphical user interface needs to be extended, but also the internal representation (representation of tuples instead of triples), together with a modification of the input and output routines. We plan to have finished a first version of the extensions to Protégé in Spring 2015 and to present it at the workshop.

[2] Depending on the application domain, these annotations might find their way as (potentially aggregated) extra arguments in the relation instances of the consequence of a rule, e.g., in (rdfp4). We will look into this in more detail at the workshop.

Acknowledgements

The research described in this paper has been partially financed by the European project PAL (Personal Assistant for healthy Lifestyle) under Grant agreement no. 643783-RIA Horizon 2020. The authors have profited from discussions with our colleague Bernd Kiefer and would like to thank the three reviewers for their suggestions.

References

Baader, F., D. Calvanese, D. McGuinness, D. Nardi, and P. Patel-Schneider (2003). *The Description Logic Handbook*. Cambridge: Cambridge University Press.

Brickley, D. and R. Guha (2014). RDF Schema 1.1. Technical report, W3C.

Calvanese, D., G. De Giacomo, and M. Lenzerini (1997). Conjunctive query containment in description logics with n-ary relations. In *Proceedings of the International Workshop on Description Logics*, pp. 5–9.

Cyganiak, R., D. Wood, and M. Lanthaler (2014). RDF 1.1 concepts and abstract syntax. Technical report, W3C.

De Giacomo, G. and M. Lenzerini (1994). Description logics with inverse roles, functional restrictions, n-ary relations. In *Proceedings of the 4th European Workshop on Logics in Artificial Intelligence*, pp. 332–346.

Hayes, P. (2004). RDF semantics. Technical report, W3C.

Hayes, P. and C. Welty (2006). Defining N-ary relations on the Semantic Web. Technical report, W3C.

Hitzler, P., M. Krötzsch, B. Parsia, P. F. Patel-Schneider, and S. Rudolph (2012). OWL 2 web ontology language primer (second edition). Technical report, W3C.

Horridge, M. (2004). A practical guide to building OWL ontologies with the Protégé-OWL plugin. Technical report, University of Manchester.

Krieger, H.-U. (2012). A temporal extension of the Hayes/ter Horst entailment rules and an alternative to W3C's n-ary relations. In *Proceedings of the 7th International Conference on Formal Ontology in Information Systems (FOIS)*, pp. 323–336.

Krieger, H.-U. (2013). An efficient implementation of equivalence relations in OWL via rule and query rewriting. In *Proceedings of the 7th IEEE International Conference on Semantic Computing (ICSC)*, pp. 260–263.

Krieger, H.-U. (2014). A detailed comparison of seven approaches for the annotation of time-dependent factual knowledge in RDF and OWL. In *Proceedings of the 10th Joint ACL-ISO Workshop on Interoperable Semantic Annotation*.

Lutz, C., U. Sattler, and S. Tobies (1999). A suggestion for an n-ary description logic. In *Proceedings of the International Workshop on Description Logics*, pp. 81–85.

Motik, B., B. Cuenca Grau, I. Horrocks, Z. Wu, A. Fokoue, and C. Lutz (2012). OWL 2 web ontology language profiles. Technical report, W3C.

Schmolze, J. G. (1989). Terminological knowledge representation systems supporting n-ary terms. In *Proceedings of the 1st International Conference on Principles of Knowledge Representation and Reasoning*, pp. 432–443.

Sider, T. (2001). *Four Dimensionalism. An Ontology of Persistence and Time*. Oxford University Press.

Smith, M. K., C. Welty, and D. L. McGuinness (2004). OWL Web Ontology Language Guide. Technical report, W3C.

ter Horst, H. J. (2005). Completeness, decidability and complexity of entailment for RDF Schema and a semantic extension involving the OWL vocabulary. *Journal of Web Semantics 3*, 79–115.

Ontology Authoring Inspired By Dialogue*

Artemis Parvizi[1], Yuan Ren[1], Markel Vigo[2], Kees van Deemter[1], Chris Mellish[1], Jeff Z. Pan[1], Robert Stevens[2] and Caroline Jay[2]

University of Aberdeen
[1]{a.parvizi, y.ren,k.vdeemter,c.mellish,jeff.z.pan}@abdn.ac.uk
University of Manchester
[2]{markel.vigo,robert.stevens,caroline.jay}@manchester.ac.uk

Abstract

This paper introduces a dialogue-based ontology authoring interface. The aim of this interface is to simplify the ontology authoring process for the users. The design of the interface is based on the insights that have emerged from research into human language and explorations of authoring activities in Protégé. We will discuss our initial findings regarding ontology authoring patterns and how we aim at modelling user's goals and intentions. We will also discuss the challenges arising whilst generating interesting and comprehensible feedback.

1 Introduction

The idea that human-computer interfaces can be seen as supporting a *dialogue* between a user and a system is well established; its origins are difficult to trace with certainty.[1] This idea has particular appeal in the case of knowledge authoring, as when a human author uses an interface such as Protégé to construct or modify a formal ontology. In knowledge authoring, the information conveyed by both the system and the user consists of potentially complex propositions instead of only button pushes or selections of an item from a menu, for example; this complexity makes the metaphor of a dialogue apt.

The present paper is an intermediate report on some parts of a project that takes the analogy between ontology authoring (OA) and human dialogue seriously by making use of insights that have emerged from research into human language. The aim is that by doing this, we will ultimately make knowledge authoring interfaces more effective, because they will offer users a better understanding of the ontologies that they produce during their interaction.

We start this exploration with an investigation of the dialogue patterns between an ontology author and their ontology in Protégé. By recording all actions at the Protégé user interface, along with the use of eye-tracking, we have a dataset that can be explored using techniques such as N-gram analysis. From this we obtain a set of typical patterns of authoring activity that are 'dialogues' between ontology author and Protégé. Based on the initial explorations of authoring activities with Protégé, we analysed the existing speech acts in Protégé and drafted a manual highlighting the potential speech acts for a dialogue-based ontology authoring interface. Section 3 will discuss this interface.

From this base, we then discuss the problem that a knowledge editing tool faces when it has to feed back to a user the effects of a knowledge editing action (e.g., the addition of an axiom to the ontology) in terms of the propositions entailed by the ontology (Section 4). We argue that this problem bears important similarities to what a Natural Language Generation system does when it selects, orders, and aggregates information for presentation to a reader, and this suggests ways in which the "entailment selection" problem in knowledge authoring might be solved.

*This work was supported by EPSRC grants EP/J014354/1 and EP/J014176/1.

[1]See e.g. various contributions in The Structure of Multimodal Dialogue, Volumes 1 and 2.

Natural language dialogues also allow the participants to discuss their current goals. In the context of ontology authoring, we interpret these as the natural language Competency Questions (CQs) that are used by many ontology authors. As questions, CQs are conversationally appropriate only when certain presuppositions (Beaver, 1997) in the CQ are satisfied by the ontology. For example, for the CQ "Which software implements some algorithm?" to be appropriate, in the ontology some software should be allowed to implement an algorithm, and some software should also be allowed to not implement an algorithm. Otherwise the answers will always be "None of them" or "Every one of them", no matter how software and algorithms are described. We analyse the patterns of CQs in practice, from which authoring tests corresponding to the presuppositions can be automatically deduced. The status of the tests (i.e., whether a given test is true or false given the ontology) can be fed back to the user in a manner that we expect to be helpful.

2 Ontology Authoring Patterns in Protégé

In order to support ontology authoring as a dialogue, we need an understanding of what speech acts are appropriate in this activity. To anchor this in reality we are carrying out an analysis of how people use an existing ontology authoring tool, even though this presents something rather different from natural language dialogue. The hope is that, at least at an abstract level, common activity patterns observed in current practice will give us ideas about functionalities to be supported by our speech acts.

The activity patterns in the ontology authoring process signal the existence of common ways of addressing the authoring tasks. These patterns are of importance as they can potentially be mapped into recommendations for the design of a user interface, for the inclusion of new functionalities or to articulate innovative interaction modalities such as the speech acts in Section 3.

In order to seek these activity patterns we instrumented Protégé, which is the preferred tool of 74% of the ontology developers according to a recent survey (Warren, 2013). Our instrumented Protégé logs the events triggered by users when authoring ontologies. These events can be classified as interaction events (e.g. expanding the class hierarchy), authoring events (e.g. add a new class) and environment events (e.g. load an ontology). Sixteen participants carried out 3 authoring tasks with the instrumented version of Protégé. Additionally we used an eye-tracker to identify how attention was allocated to different areas of Protégé. The log files collected contained a mean of $\sim$7K rows of events, which accounted for 45 minutes of interaction.

In analysing these log files, we first removed those events that were not meaningful: i.e. the invocation of the reasoner generates several events that can be summarised into one, namely *reasoner invoked.* Second, those events that were infrequent and had been triggered anecdotally were removed (i.e. use of the search functionality). Third, we carried out an analysis of N-grams in order to find the patterns in these long sequences of events. We discovered that the most frequent N-grams were those repeating the same event: i.e. *entity select, entity select, entity select ....* To more readily reveal authoring patterns, we merged all the N-grams containing the same events. In the above example the merging led to new multiple events such as *multiple entity select.* After the merging, the higher-level activities include:

- The **exploration** activity describes how users navigate an unfamiliar ontology, and the different exploration patterns in the asserted and the inferred hierarchy. While in the former users try to find a specific location in the hierarchy in order to add or modify a class, in the latter the behaviour is more of an exploratory nature and is often related to checking the consequences of running the reasoner.
- The **editing** activity indicates how properties are added to classes and how restrictions are established on them by selecting an entity in the class hierarchy, looking at the description window and invoking the entity modification window.
- Often, saving the ontology initiates the **reasoning** activity, which is followed by the exploration of the inferred hierarchy to ascertain how the hierarchy has been updated by the automated reasoner.

The method we are using for this activity is essentially the same as using corpus analysis to inform the design of a natural language dialogue system, the only difference being that the low level dialogue moves being observed are in this case button clicks and keyboard events, rather than natural language utterances.

3 A Dialogue Interface for Ontology Authoring

As a step towards the construction of a dialogue-based interface, the WHATIF gadget, we have drafted an authoring manual, a set of speech acts for Protégé, and a dialogue manual containing dialogue speech acts[2] (Parvizi et al., 2013). Based on these manuals and Nielsen's (Nielsen, 1986) proposed model of human computer interaction[3], we have developed a prototype of a dialogue system. In the latest version of the prototype, speech acts *a*) checking, *b*) observation, *c*) axiom addition, *d*) modelling element addition[4], *e*) axiom or modelling element deletion, *f*) axiom modification, and *g*) WHATIF question have been implemented. The system presents this list of speech acts to the users and requires them to select one. In addition, deletion and modification speech acts, the normal process of ontology authoring is carried out; the *checking* speech act will inform the user of the presence or absence of a specific modelling element or an axiom; the *observation* speech act provides a detailed account of the characteristic of a specific modelling element or an axiom; and importantly, the WHATIF speech act in which the user can ask a question about the logical consequences of an authoring action, and the system will perform a look-ahead search and provide a description of changes and future implications.

Based on the analysis done in Section 2, we can map *(1)* observation to exploration, *(2)* checking to a combination of reasoning and exploration *(3)* adding, deleting, and modifying to editing, and *(4)* WHATIF to a combination of reasoning and exploration activities.

The WHATIF gadget receives users' requests in Manchester syntax or OSE along with a speech act; the command is parsed and, based on the speech act, an appropriate response is generated. The next step is to use the coherence and relevance between various commands to provide an unambiguous and clear feedback or occasionally summarise the generated responses (see Section 4). We also aim at simplifying the ontology authoring process by understanding users' goals and intention (see Section 5).
Users interact with the system through the following panels:

Class hierarchy: panel displays the *inferred* hierarchy to the users. This hierarchy is updated after each editing task (adding, removing, and modifying), and the user can always view the current state of the ontology.

Class description: this panel will be activated by clicking on any class in the class hierarchy. The panel will display the characteristics of the selected class in natural language. This panel essentially works as a verbaliser.

Input panel: this panel allows the users to enter their commands either in Manchester Syntax or in OSE. The interaction is governed by the speech acts mentioned above.

Task list: this panel contains the goals and intentions of the users, formulated as a set of competency questions (CQ). Based on each CQ, the system will generate a set of appropriate authoring tests (AT) (see Section 5). The state of each AT, pass or fail, is known by the colour of the icon, green or red.

History panel: this panel records the entire interaction between the user and the system. All the system's written feedback will appear in this panel. Also, the written status of the CQs will appear in this panel. The biggest issue is the length of the feedback provided, which will be discussed in Section 4.

---

[2] The dialogue manual was generated from an examination of existing dialogue systems and their speech acts, and a manual exploration of Protégé.

[3] Nielsen's interaction model is a dual model of the user and the computer at the same time. In this model, the interaction between the two participants, human and computer, has been viewed as a dialogue. However, unlike a human-human interaction, the two participants do not have the same communication skills. The user model has to be psychologically valid, whilst the system model has to follow some design principles.

[4] The users need to define the modelling elements (i.e classes and individuals) before they can add an axiom to the ontology.

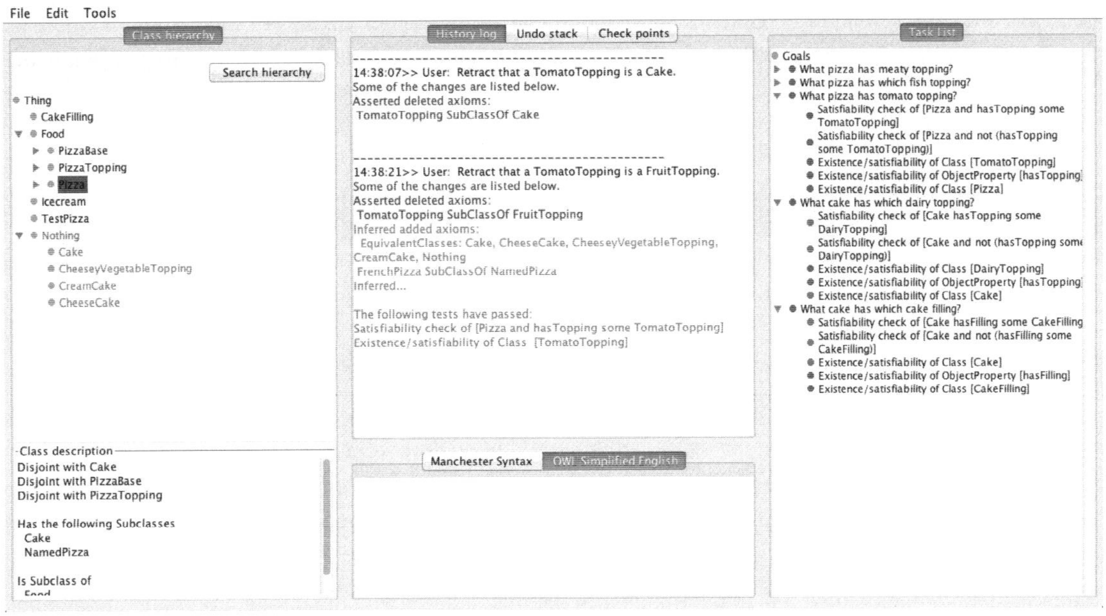

Figure 1: The WHATIF gadget

4 Giving Feedback

A real dialogue, rather than a monologue, has significant contributions from both participants. Given the knowledge-rich nature of ontology authoring, there is an opportunity to go beyond the user-driven monologues of most user interfaces by having the system provide *feedback*. In particular, an ontology author needs to be made aware of the consequences of their authoring actions. If the author has just added or deleted an axiom from the ontology, the system should tell them about the new *entailments* (the new propositions that follow from the revised axioms, and also those propositions that are no longer entailed). In some families of OWL, this set of entailments can be *infinite*, and in others large. At this step, most of the ontology authoring tools or reasoners, based on some predefined criteria, decide to show only a *subset* of these entailments. We have categorised entailment selection in previous work into the following categories:

Syntax-driven: selection is based on the explicit structure of the entailments. For instance, a syntactic approach might select axioms of the form $A \sqsubseteq B$ where A is a named concept. Such an approach is quite common in traditional ontology authoring interfaces such as Protégé which displays information based on the structural forms that the user selects. In the Rabbit to OWL Ontology authoring (ROO) editor (Denaux et al., 2012) the existence of an infinite entailment set has been acknowledged and is tackled by including only new and lost entailments of the form $A \sqsubseteq B$, $\top \sqsubseteq B$, $A \sqsubseteq \top$ and $A(a)$, where A and B are concept expressions that appear in some axiom and a is a named individual. This is probably the least restrictive syntactic approach in current use.

Logic-driven: selection is based on logical behaviour or preference (Siberski et al., 2006) of entailments. Such an approach can only make choices between axioms which are logically distinct. For example, selecting the *most specific* entailments (Mellish and Pan, 2008).

Mellish and Pan (2008) considered various logical principles based on the Gricean maxims (Grice, 1970) of cooperative conversation, places where a reader is likely to draw false implicatures where words such as "all" and "not" are used. This is beginning to go beyond a purely logical problem to a problem where the mode of presentation (here, natural language) also plays a role. That is, the maxims only apply if the interaction is regarded as a cooperative conversation of the kind conducted by people. Given our context of authoring inspired by natural dialogue, this extra assumption is especially relevant. Indeed, it suggests that there may also be useful criteria of the following kinds:

Discourse-driven: selection is based on the structure of the dialogue. Instead of viewing each interaction in isolation, we can analyse a *sequence of utterances*, and based on some criteria such as the Gricean maxim of relevance or the user's previous focus of attention, select a subset of entailments. Unlike ours, most ontology editors do not have an explicit linear discourse within which relevance and coherence arise. However, verbalisers often focus on grouping and ordering of textual material generated from ontologies. It might be possible to transform these grouping and ordering strategies into selection strategies.

Pragmatics-driven: selection is based on the user's goals and intentions. Entailment selection must potentially be customised to consider the user's aims during the authoring process. In the context of a dialogue, we might expect the user to tell us something of their goals. To this end, we introduce the notion of Competency Questions, which will be discussed in detail in Section 5.

We can see abstract similarities in design between existing authoring tools that attempt to provide feedback or generate summaries and natural language generation (NLG) systems. NLG systems are frequently based on a pipeline such as: *a*) content selection *b*) aggregation *c*) grouping and ordering Following the NLG pipeline, after content selection, we must consider grouping and ordering. Often, in ontology authoring interfaces, the order in which the entailed axioms are presented is arbitrary. Regardless of how well the entailment selection strategy has functioned, a poor ordering and grouping policy can cancel the effect of selection. We can learn a lot from verbalisers such as OntoVerbal (Liang et al., 2011), and NaturalOWL (Androutsopoulos et al., 2013). In OntoVerbal, a distinction between direct and indirect axioms is made, and in NaturalOWL, coherence and complexity of axioms play a role. But there are complex issues here, especially if entailments involving complex classes are considered.

From our survey of the literature, we conclude that there are few good logic-driven approaches to entailment selection. Therefore, for our interface we plan to investigate the syntactic selection method of Denaux et al. (2012), together with a preference ordering based on linear discourse structure and the user's goals, as represented by "Competency Questions" (Section 5).

5 Being Sensitive to the User's Goals

In natural language dialogues, the participants are aware of and sensitive to one anothers' goals. We believe this sensitivity is something that could benefit ontology authoring. Although many real world ontologies, including some of the biggest ones, are constructed manually by human authors, manual ontology authoring remains a challenging task for ontology engineers (Rector et al., 2004; Dzbor et al., 2006). A large part of the difficulty is that authors cannot easily express their requirements for the ontology and, even where this is possible, it is unclear how to check whether the requirements are fulfilled.

To tackle this problem, we are incorporating the technique of Competency Question-driven Ontology Authoring (CQOA) (Ren et al., 2014) into our dialogue system. This new technique takes "Competency Questions" as requirements for ontologies and uses them to automatically generate authoring tests for ensuring the quality of the ontology.

(Informal) Competency Questions (CQs) are expressions of natural language questions that an ontology must be able to answer (Uschold et al., 1996). Below is a typical CQ:

$$\text{Which processes implement an algorithm?} \qquad (1)$$

Obviously one can think of many other CQs with similar syntactic forms, such as "Which pizza has tomato topping?", "Which animal has a tail?". In fact, they all have the following semi-formal pattern:

$$Which\ [CE1]\ [OPE]\ [CE2]? \qquad (2)$$

where $CE1$ and $CE2$ are class expressions (or individual expressions as a special case) and OPE is a binary object property expression. Given a CQ of a particular pattern, its elements and their features can be identified.

The ability to answer a CQ meaningfully can be regarded as a *functional requirement* that must be satisfied by the ontology. We argue that for a CQ to be meaningful, its presuppositions (Beaver, 1997) must be satisfied by the ontology when the query is eventually asked. Otherwise the CQ or its answers will be trivial. For example, in order for question (1) to be meaningfully asked, the ontology must satisfy the following presuppositions:

1. Classes $Process$, $Algorithm$ and property $implements$ occur in the ontology;
2. The ontology allows the possibility of $Process$es implementing *Algorithms*;
3. The ontology allows the possibility of $Process$es *not* implementing $Algorithm$s.

Particularly, if case 2 was not satisfied, the ontology could never have any $Process$ implementing any $Algorithm$ and the answer to the CQ is always "none". This would be exactly the kind of uncooperative answer looked at by the previous work on cooperative question-answering (Gaasterland et al., 1992). It is hard to imagine an ontology author really wanting to retrieve this information. Rather, this can be taken as evidence of possible design problems in the ontology. If case 3 was not satisfied, the answer to all the $Algorithms$ would be a list of all the $Process$es. This would mean that the questions would be similarly uninteresting to the ontology author, again signalling a possible problem in the ontology.

With the corresponding features and elements, the presuppositions of a certain CQ pattern can be formally represented and verified. For example, the presuppositions shown above for CQ pattern (2) can be verified automatically: (1) $CE1$, $CE2$ and OPE should occur in the ontology; (2) The class expression $CE1$ *and* (OPE *some* $CE2$) should be satisfiable in the ontology; (3) The class expression $CE1$ *and not* (OPE *some* $CE2$) should also be satisfiable in the ontology. Such kind of tests that can be derived from CQs are called *Authoring Tests* (ATs). All ATs in CQOA can be automatically tested.

This CQOA pipeline has been integrated in the interface presented in Section 3. CQs are either imported into the interface, or are entered by the users. The system will analyse CQs and identify their elements and patterns, based on which corresponding ATs will be generated and tested against the ontology. The status of ATs are constantly being monitored by the reasoner, and reported to the user. As seen in Figure 3, a traffic light approach for pass or fail status in the "task list" panel, and a written feedback in the "history log" panel will inform user of the status of the ATs. For the sake of conciseness of the interface, one can provide feedback only when the status of an AT has changed.

6 Discussion and Outlook

The WHATIF project explores what we take to be a few big ideas.

- **First of all**, we envision that understanding dialogue patterns between ontology authors and their editing tools could help improve ontology authoring tools, in particular for those providing a dialogue interface (Section 3). Our research indicates the existence of activity patterns for ontology authors using Protégé, a well known ontology editing tool (Section 2).
- **Secondly**, we advocate test-driven ontology authoring. An ontology should not just contain OWL files, but also other artefacts, such as competency questions and authoring tests. Research suggests that there exist a limited number of syntactic patterns for competency questions and these questions can be used as ontology requirements to generate authoring tests (Section 5). This means that ontology authors can use some controlled natural languages to specify their competency questions.
- **Thirdly**, we envision that dialogue based ontology authoring can get benefits from research into human language. For example, the 'entailment selection' problem in ontology authoring bears important similarities to what a Natural Language Generation system does for information presentation to a reader (Section 4).

As for future work, we plan to perform further evaluations. In an experiment that we plan to perform soon, participants will be asked to fulfil a task that involves over and underspecified parts in an ontology. We will measure the performance of users in the presence or absence of authoring tests. We will also measure the usefulness of the visual/written feedback given to the users. In a separate evaluation we will also evaluate the axiom selection mechanism during a predefined set of authoring tasks.

References

Androutsopoulos, I., G. Lampouras, and D. Galanis (2013). Generating natural language descriptions from OWL ontologies: the NaturalOWL system. *Journal of AI Research 48*, 671–715.

Beaver, D. (1997). Presupposition. In J. van Benthem and A. ter Meulen (Eds.), *The Handbook of Logic and Language*, pp. 939–1008. Elsevier.

Denaux, R., D. Thakker, V. Dimitrova, and A. G. Cohn (2012). Interactive Semantic Feedback for Intuitive Ontology Authoring. In *FOIS*, pp. 160–173.

Dzbor, M., E. Motta, J. M. Gomez, C. Buil, K. Dellschaft, O. Görlitz, and H. Lewen (2006, August). D4.1.1 Analysis of user needs, behaviours & requirements wrt user interfaces for ontology engineering. Technical report, Intelligent Software Components (ISOCO).

Gaasterland, T., P. Godfrey, and J. Minker (1992). An overview of cooperative answering. *Journal of Intelligent Information Systems 1*(2), 123–157.

Grice, H. P. (1970). *Logic and conversation.* Harvard Univ.

Liang, S. F., R. Stevens, D. Scott, and A. Rector (2011). Automatic verbalisation of SNOMED classes using ontoverbal. In *Artificial Intelligence in Medicine*, pp. 338–342. Springer.

Mellish, C. and J. Z. Pan (2008). Natural language directed inference from ontologies. *Artificial Intelligence 172*(10), 1285–1315.

Nielsen, J. (1986). A virtual protocol model for computer-human interaction. *International Journal of Man-Machine Studies 24*(3), 301–312.

Parvizi, A., C. Jay, C. Mellish, J. Z. Pan, Y. Ren, R. Stevens, and K. van Deemter (2013). A pilot experiment in knowledge authoring as dialogue. In *ISWC, Potsdam, Germany*.

Rector, A., N. Drummond, M. Horridge, J. Rogers, H. Knublauch, R. Stevens, H. Wang, and C. Wroe (2004). OWL pizzas: Practical experience of teaching OWL-DL: Common errors & common patterns. pp. 63–81. Springer.

Ren, Y., A. Parvizi, C. Mellish, J. Z. Pan, K. van Deemter, and R. Stevens. (2014). Towards competency question-driven ontology authoring. In *Proc. of ESWC 2014*.

Siberski, W., J. Z. Pan, and U. Thaden (2006). Querying the Semantic Web with Preferences. In *In Proc. of the 5th International Semantic Web Conference (ISWC2006)*, pp. 612 – 624.

Uschold, M., M. Gruninger, et al. (1996). Ontologies: Principles, methods and applications. *Knowledge engineering review 11*(2), 93–136.

Warren, P. (2013). Ontology users' survey – summary of results. Technical Report Technical Report KMI-13-1, Knowledge Media Institute.

Parsing Software Requirements with an Ontology-based Semantic Role Labeler

Michael Roth
University of Edinburgh
mroth@inf.ed.ac.uk

Ewan Klein
University of Edinburgh
ewan@inf.ed.ac.uk

Abstract

Software requirements describe functional and non-functional aspects of a software system and form the basis for the development process. Accordingly, requirements of existing systems can provide insights regarding the re-usability of already implemented software artifacts. To facilitate direct comparison between requirements of existing and to be developed systems, we propose to automatically map requirements in natural language text to structured semantic representations. For this task, we adapt techniques from semantic role labeling to a high-level ontology that defines concepts and relations for describing static software functionalities. The proposed method achieves a precision and recall of 77.9% and 74.5%, respectively, on an annotated software requirements dataset and significantly outperforms two baselines that are based on lexical and syntactic patterns.

1 Introduction

During the process of software development, developers and customers typically discuss and agree on requirements that specify the functionality of a system that is being developed.[1] Such requirements play a crucial role in the development lifecycle, as they form the basis for implementations, corresponding work plans, cost estimations and follow-up directives (van Lamsweerde, 2009). In general, software requirements can be expressed in various different ways, including the use of UML diagrams and storyboards. Most commonly, however, expectations are expressed in natural language (Mich et al., 2004), as shown in Example (1):

(1) A user should be able to login to his account.

While requirements expressed in natural language have the advantage of being intelligible to both clients and developers, they can of course also be ambiguous, vague and incomplete. Although formal languages could be used as an alternative that eliminates some of these problems, customers are rarely equipped with the mathematical and technical expertise for understanding highly formalised requirements. To benefit from the advantages of both natural language and formal representations, we propose to induce the latter automatically from text in a semantic parsing task. Given the software requirement in Example (1), for instance, we would like to construct a representation that explicitly specifies the types of the entities involved (e.g., OBJECT(account)) and relationships among them (e.g., ACTS_ON(login, account)).

Though there exist ontologies and small-scale data sets with annotated concept instances, most previous approaches to inducing such annotations from text relied on hand-crafted grammars and heuristic postprocessing rules. In this paper, we propose to identify and classify instances of ontology concepts and relations using statistical techniques from semantic role labeling.

The remainder of this paper is structured as follows. In Section 2, we describe previous approaches on converting software requirements to formal representations. In Section 3, we provide a summary

[1] Although software engineering can also involve *non-functional* requirements, which describe general quality criteria of a system, this paper is only concerned with functional requirements, i.e., requirements that specify the behavior of a system.

of a previously developed ontology and annotated data set which we use for training and testing our own approach. In Section 4, we decribe the semantic role labeling architecture that we developed to automatically process software requirements. In Section 5, we evaluate our proposed approach and compare it to two pattern-based baselines. Finally, we conclude this paper in Section 6 with a discussion and outlook on future work.

2 Related Work

A range of methods have been proposed in previous work to (semi-)automatically process requirements written in plain, natural language text and map them to formal representations. To the best of our knowledge, Abbott (1983) was the first to introduce a technique for extracting data types, variables and operators from informal texts describing a problem. The proposed method follows a simple rule-based setup, in which common nouns are identified as data types, proper nouns as objects and verbs as operators between them. Booch (1986) described a method of similar complexity that extends Abbot's approach to object-oriented development. Saeki et al. (1989) implemented a first prototype that automatically constructs object-oriented models from informal requirements. As proposed by Abbott and Booch, the system is based on automatically extracted nouns and verbs. Although Saeki et al. found resulting object diagrams of reasonable quality, they concluded that human intervention was still necessary to distinguish between words that are relevant for the model and irrelevant nouns and verbs. Nanduri and Rugaber (1995) proposed to further automate object-oriented analysis of requirement texts by applying a syntactic parser and a set of post-processing rules. In a similar setting, Mich (1996) employed a full NLP pipeline that contains a semantic analysis module, thus omitting the need for additional post-processing rules. More recent approaches include those by Harmain and Gaizauskas (2003) and Kof (2004), who relied on a combination of NLP components and human interaction. Whereas most previous approaches aim to derive class diagrams, Ghosh et al. (2014) proposed a pipeline architecture that induces logical expressions from syntactic parses via a set of heuristic post-processing rules.

Despite this seemingly long tradition, methods for processing software requirements have tended to depend on domain-specific heuristics and knowledge bases or have required additional user intervention. In contrast, we propose to utilize annotated data to learn how to perform semantic parsing of requirements automatically.

3 Ontology and Dataset

As training and testing material for our semantic role labeling approach, we use a high-level ontology of static software functionalities and an existing data set of software requirements with annotated ontology instances (Roth et al., 2014). The ontology by Roth et al. covers general concepts for describing static software functionalities. The main concepts and their associated relations are as follows:

`Action` An `Action` describes an operation that is performed by an `Actor` on any number of `Object(s)`.[2] The participants of an `Action` are indicated by the relations HAS_ACTOR and ACTS_ON, respectively.

`Actor` (HAS_ACTOR) A `Actor` is an active participant of an `Action` and can be the user of a system or a software system itself.

`Object` (ACTS_ON) A `Object` is any kind of entity involved in an `Action` other than the `Actor`.

`Property` (HAS_PROPERTY) A `Property` is an attribute of an `Object`, a characteristic of an `Action` or an optional specification of an `Actor`. The domain of the relation HAS_PROPERTY will be the set of entities which possess a given `Property`.

[2]Note that an `Action` is a kind of entity, so the approach is similar to a Davidsonian event-based semantics.

Concept	Instances	Relations	Instances
Action	435		
Actor	305	HAS_ACTOR	355
Object	613	ACTS_ON	531
Property	698	HAS_PROPERTY	690
Total	2,051	Total	1,576

Table 1: Counts of annotated instances of concepts and relations in the dataset from Roth et al. (2014)

The annotated data is based on a collection of functional software requirements from software engineering classes at universities and industrial prototypes of a software company (for details, cf. Roth et al., 2014).[3] The collection contains 325 requirement sentences, over 2,000 annotated instances of ontology concepts and more than 1,500 instances of relations between concepts. All annotations refer to concepts and relations described in the previous paragraphs. Table 1 provides counts of annotations per concept and relation type. Note that instances of `Actor` can be involved in multiple instances of `Action` and some instances of `Object` are not involved in any, hence the number of relations can differ from the number of associated concepts. Since all annotations are provided as mark-up for tokens in text, we can directly use the annotated data set for our role labeling approach, which we describe in the next section.

4 Ontology-based Semantic Role Labeling

The goal of this work is to automatically identify and extract instances of ontology concepts and relations from software requirements expressed in natural language text. Based on the ontology and dataset described in Section 3, we developed a parser that learns statistical models for this task and can be applied to new data. In practice, the parsing task involves several steps: first, instances of concepts need to be identified and then mapped to the correct class and second, relations between instances of concepts need to be identified and labeled accordingly.

Inspired by previous work on semantic role labeling, we use a parsing pipeline consisting of a syntactic dependency parser and several semantic analyses modules. We specifically chose this kind of architecture as our task closely resembles previous semantic role labeling (SRL) tasks, in which such systems achieve state-of-the-art performance (Hajič et al., 2009). To meet the constraints and characteristics of the software requirements domain, we have taken as our starting point techniques for labeling roles of the kind standardly used in domain-independent semantic analyses and extended them to the concepts and relations defined in the ontology (cf. Section 3).

The following subsections describe our implementation in more detail. In Section 4.1, we introduce the preprocessing pipeline that we apply to compute a syntactic analysis for each requirement expressed as a sentence in English. Section 4.2 describes the semantic analysis modules that we implemented to map words and constituents in a sentence to instances of concepts and relations from the ontology. Finally, we define the features and learning techniques applied to train each statistical model in subsections 4.3. We illustrate each step of our analysis using the following running examples:

(a) "The user must be able to upload photos."

(b) "Any user must be able to search by tag the public bookmarks of all RESTMARKS users."

4.1 Syntactic Analysis

The syntactic analysis stage of our pipeline architecture consists of the following steps: tokenization, part-of-speech tagging, lemmatization and dependency parsing. Given an input sentence, this means that

[3] We thank the authors for making their data available to us.

the pipeline separates the sentence into word tokens, identifies the grammatical category of each word (e.g., "user" → noun, "upload" → verb) and determines their uninflected base forms (e.g., "users" → "user"). Finally, the pipeline identifies syntactic dependents of each word and their respective grammatical relation (e.g., ⟨"user","must"⟩ → subject-of, ⟨"upload","photos"⟩ → object-of).

For all syntactic analysis steps, we rely on components and pre-trained models from a system called Mate tools (Björkelund et al., 2010; Bohnet, 2010), which is freely available online.[4] This choice is based on two criteria. First, the system achieves state-of-the-art performance on a benchmark data set for syntactic analysis (Hajič et al., 2009). Second, the output of the syntactic analysis steps has successfully been used as input for the related task of PropBank/NomBank-style semantic role labeling (Palmer et al., 2005; Meyers et al., 2008).

4.2 Semantic Analysis

Our actual semantic role labeling pipeline consists of four main steps to extract instances of ontology concepts and relations from requirements written in natural language text: (1) identifying instances of the concepts `Action` and `Object`, (2) assigning the respective concept type, (3) determining instances of related concepts, and (4) labeling relationships between pairs of concept instances. Our implementation is based on the semantic role labeler from Mate tools and uses the built-in re-ranker to find the best joint output of steps (3) and (4). We extend Mate tools with respect to continuous features and arbitrary label types. We describe each component of our implementation in the following paragraphs.

Step (1) The first component of our pipeline identifies words in a text that instantiate the ontology concepts `Action` and `Object`. The motivation for identifying these two concept types first is that only they govern relationships to all other ontology concepts through the three relations ACTS_ON, HAS_ACTOR and HAS_PROPERTY. We hence expect the corresponding linguistic units to behave similarly to PropBank/NomBank predicates and can apply similar features as used in the *predicate identification* step implemented in Mate tools. Our implementation considers each verb and each noun in a sentence and performs binary classification based on lexical semantic and syntactic properties.

Step (2) This step determines which ontology concept is applicable to each instance identified in Step (1). That is, for each verb and noun in a sentence classified as a potential instance of `Action` and `Object`, the component predicts and instantiates the actual ontology concept (e.g., "upload"→`action`, "search"→`action`). As in the previous component, lexical semantic and syntactic properties are exploited to perform classification. This step corresponds to the *predicate disambiguation* step applied in PropBank/NomBank semantic role labeling but, in contrast to the former, the available set of labels is predefined in the ontology and hence does not depend on the identified "predicate".

Step (3) The component for determining related concept instances detects words and phrases in a text that are related to the instances previously identified in Step (1). The main goal of this step is to identify the `Actor` of an `Action` and affected `Objects` as well as instances of `Property` that are related to any of the former. As such, this step is similar to *argument identification* in semantic role labeling. Accordingly, we take as input potential 'arguments' of a concept instance from Step (1) and perform binary decisions that indicate whether a word or phrase instantiates a (related) ontology concept. In example (a), both "the user" and "photos" are ontology instances that are related to the `Action` expressed by the word "upload". In example (b), instances related to "search" are: "any user", "by tag" and "the public bookmarks of all RESTMARKS users". In this example, "of all RESTMARKS users" further denotes a `Property` related to the instance of `Object` expressed by the phrase "the public bookmarks".

[4] `http://code.google.com/p/mate-tools/`

	Action and Object identification	Action and Object classification	Related concepts identification	Related concepts classification
Affected word forms	•	•	•	•
Affected word lemmata	•	–	–	–
Word part-of-speech	•	–	•	•
Word vector representation	•	•	•	•
Relation to parent	•	–	•	•
Parent part-of-speech	•	•	–	–
Set of dependent relations	–	•	–	–
Single child words	•	–	–	–
Single child part-of-speech	•	–	–	–
Dependencies between words	–	–	•	•
Order of affected words	–	–	•	•
Distance between words	–	–	•	–

Table 2: Linguistic properties that are used as features in statistical classification

Step (4) The component for labeling relationships determines which relations hold between a pair of ontology instances as identified in Steps (1) and (3). Generally, each instance can be involved in multiple relations and hence more than one concept type can apply to a single entity. To represent this circumstance appropriately, the component performs classification on pairs of related instances (e.g., ⟨"the user", "upload"⟩ → ⟨Actor, Action⟩, ⟨"by tag", "search"⟩ → ⟨Property, Action⟩). This step roughly corresponds to the *argument classification* step of the semantic role labeler implemented in Mate tools. As with concept labels, however, our set of potential relations is predefined in the ontology. For classification, our implementation relies on lexical semantic and syntactic properties as well as additional characteristics that hold between the linguistic expressions that refer to the considered instances (e.g., their order in text).

4.3 Features and Learning

In practice, each step in our pipeline is implemented as a logistic regression model that uses linguistic properties as features, for which appropriate features weights are learned based on annotated training data. The majority of features applied in our models are already implemented in Mate tools (Björkelund et al., 2010). Given that the number of annotations available for our task is about one order of magnitude smaller than those in PropBank/NomBank, we utilize a subset of features from previous work, as summarized in Table 2, which we greedily selected based on classification performance.

To compensate for sparse features in our setting, we define additional features based on distributional semantics. The motivation for such features lies in the fact that indicator features and feature combinations (e.g., the affected word type plus its part-of-speech) can be too specific to provide robust generalization for semantic analysis. To overcome the resulting gap in coverage, we represent each word in a classification decision by a low-rank vector representation that is computed based on word-context co-occurrence counts and can be computed over large amounts of unlabeled text. As distributional representations tends to be similar for words that are similar in meaning, this allows word type information to be utilized at test time, even if a specific word has not occurred in the training data.

As indicated in Table 2, we apply vector representations of words for identifying instances of Action and Object as well as for classifying instances of related concepts. Following a recent comparison of different word representations for semantic role labeling (Roth and Woodsend, 2014), we use a set of publicly available vectors that were learned using a neural language model (Bengio et al., 2003).[5]

[5] http://github.com/turian/neural-language-model

Model	Precision	Recall	F_1-score
Baseline 1 (word-level patterns)	62.8	35.2	45.1
Baseline 2 (syntax-based patterns)	78.3	62.1	69.3
Full SRL model	77.9	74.5	76.2

Table 3: Performance of our full model and two simplified baselines; all numbers in %

5 Evaluation

We evaluate the performance of the semantic role labeling approach described in Section 4, using the annotated dataset described in Section 3. As evaluation metrics, we apply labeled precision and recall. We define *labeled precision* as the fraction of predicted labels of concept and relation instances that are correct, and *labeled recall* as the fraction of annotated labels that are correctly predicted by the parser. To train and test the statistical models underlying the semantic analysis components of our pipeline, we perform evaluation in a 5-fold cross-validation setting. That is, given the 325 sentences from the annotated data set, we randomly create five folds of equal size (65 sentences) and use each fold once for testing while training on the remaining other folds.

As baselines, we apply two pattern-based models that are similar in spirit to earlier approaches to parsing software requirements (cf. Section 2). The first baseline simply uses word level patterns to identify instances of ontology concepts and relations. The second baseline is similar to the first but also takes into account syntactic relationships between potential instances of ontology concepts. For simplicity, we train both baseline models using the same architecture as our proposed method but only use a sub-set of the applied features. In the first baseline, we only apply features indicating word forms, lemmata and parts-of-speech as well as the order between words. For the second baseline, we use all features from the first baseline plus indicator features on syntactic relationships between words that potentially instantiate ontology concepts.

The results of both baselines and our full semantic role labeling model are summarized in Table 3. Using all features described in Section 4.3, our model achieves a precision and recall of 77.9% and 74.5%, respectively. The corresponding F_1-score, calculated as the harmonic mean between precision and recall, is 76.2%. The baselines only achieve F_1-scores of 45.1% and 69.3%, respectively. A significance test based on random approximate shuffling (Yeh, 2000) confirmed that the differences in results between our model and each baseline is statistically significant ($p<0.01$).

6 Conclusions

We conclude this paper with an outlook on how the work presented here contributes to computer-assisted software engineering. The main aim of the latter is to semi-automate the process of getting from software specifications to actual implementations. Ontologies and semantically annotated requirements can help achieve this goal by providing a meaningful and structured representations of software components. To truly assist software engineering, the mapping from requirements to ontology instances needs to be performed computationally. Towards this goal, we developed a semantic role labeling approach that automatically induces ontology-based representations from text. Our model achieves a high precision on this task and significantly outperforms two pattern-based baselines. In future work, we will empirically validate the usefulness of our proposed approach in downstream applications.

Acknowledgements

Parts of this work have been supported by the FP7 Collaborative Project S-CASE (Grant Agreement No 610717), funded by the European Commission.

References

Abbott, R. J. (1983). Program design by informal English descriptions. *Communications of the ACM 26*(11), 882–894.

Bengio, Y., R. Ducharme, P. Vincent, and C. Jauvin (2003). A neural probabilistic language model. *Journal of Machine Learning Research 3*, 1137–1155.

Björkelund, A., B. Bohnet, L. Hafdell, and P. Nugues (2010). A high-performance syntactic and semantic dependency parser. In *Coling 2010: Demonstration Volume*, Beijing, China, pp. 33–36.

Bohnet, B. (2010). Top accuracy and fast dependency parsing is not a contradiction. In *Proceedings of the 23rd International Conference on Computational Linguistics*, Beijing, China, pp. 89–97.

Booch, G. (1986). Object-oriented development. *IEEE Transactions on Software Engineering* (2), 211–221.

Ghosh, S., D. Elenius, W. Li, P. Lincoln, N. Shankar, and W. Steiner (2014). Automatically extracting requirements specifications from natural language. *arXiv preprint arXiv:1403.3142*.

Hajič, J., M. Ciaramita, R. Johansson, D. Kawahara, M. A. Martí, L. Màrquez, A. Meyers, J. Nivre, S. Padó, J. Štěpánek, et al. (2009). The CoNLL-2009 shared task: Syntactic and semantic dependencies in multiple languages. In *Proceedings of the Thirteenth Conference on Computational Natural Language Learning: Shared Task*, pp. 1–18.

Harmain, H. M. and R. Gaizauskas (2003). Cm-builder: A natural language-based case tool for object-oriented analysis. *Automated Software Engineering 10*(2), 157–181.

Kof, L. (2004). Natural language processing for requirements engineering: Applicability to large requirements documents. In *19th International Conference on Automated Software Engineering, Workshop Proceedings*.

Meyers, A., R. Reeves, and C. Macleod (2008). *NomBank v1.0.* Linguistic Data Consortium, Philadelphia.

Mich, L. (1996). NL-OOPS: From natural language to object oriented requirements using the natural language processing system LOLITA. *Natural Language Engineering 2*(2), 161–187.

Mich, L., F. Mariangela, and N. I. Pierluigi (2004). Market research for requirements analysis using linguistic tools. *Requirements Engineering 9*(1), 40–56.

Nanduri, S. and S. Rugaber (1995). Requirements validation via automated natural language parsing. In *Proceedings of the Twenty-Eighth Hawaii International Conference on System Sciences*, Volume 3, pp. 362–368.

Palmer, M., D. Gildea, and P. Kingsbury (2005). The Proposition bank: An annotated corpus of semantic roles. *Computational Linguistics 31*(1), 71–106.

Roth, M., T. Diamantopoulos, E. Klein, and A. Symeonidis (2014). Software requirements: A new domain for semantic parsers. In *Proceedings of the ACL 2014 Workshop on Semantic Parsing*, Baltimore, Maryland, USA, pp. 50–54.

Roth, M. and K. Woodsend (2014). Composition of word representations improves semantic role labelling. In *Proceedings of the 2014 Conference on Empirical Methods in Natural Language Processing*, Doha, Qatar, pp. 407–413.

Saeki, M., H. Horai, and H. Enomoto (1989). Software development process from natural language specification. In *Proceedings of the 11th International Conference on Software Engineering*, pp. 64–73.

van Lamsweerde, A. (2009). *Requirements Engineering: From System Goals to UML Models to Software Specifications*. Wiley.

Yeh, A. (2000). More accurate tests for the statistical significance of result differences. In *Proceedings of the 18th International Conference on Computational Linguistics*, Saarbrücken, Germany, pp. 947–953.

Using Ontologies to Model Polysemy in Lexical Resources

Fahad Khan[1] and Francesca Frontini[1, 2]

[1]Istituto di Linguistica Computazionale "A. Zampolli" , CNR Pisa
[2]Laboratoire d'informatique de Paris 6 , Labex OBVIL , Paris
firstname.secondname@ilc.cnr.it

Abstract

In this article we look at how the use of ontologies can assist in analysing polysemy in natural languages. We develop a model, the Lexical-Sense-Ontology model (LSO), to represent the interaction between a lexicon and ontology, based on *lemon*. We use the LSO model to show how default rules can be used to represent semi-productivity in polysemy as well as discussing the kinds of ontological information that are useful for studying polysemy.

1 Introduction

Given the current high levels of interest in lingustic linked open data and the availability of large scale, wide coverage ontologies like DBpedia and SUMO it was inevitable that there should also be an increased focus on the idea of using computational ontologies to provide semantic information for lexical resources, especially within the context of the Semantic Web. In this article we look at different ways in which ontologies and ontological knowledge can potentially help to describe and analyse the semantic phenomena of polysemy. Arguably the most popular RDF based model for linking together lexica with ontologies for the purpose of describing word meaning is *lemon* (Mccrae et al. (2012)). The *lemon* model is based on the principle of *semantics by reference* which foresees a clear separation of lexical and ontological layers in a lexico-semantic resource, using reified sense objects to map between the two, and argues for the semantics of a lexicon being wholly contained within the ontology (see Cimiano et al. (2013)). Our approach in this article is also based on a clear lexicon-ontology distinction in which senses are regarded as interfacing between lexical and ontological layers, as is posited in *lemon*. We will introduce our own model, the Lexicon-Sense-Ontology model (LSO) which is closely based on *lemon* (but which doesn't necessarily deal only with lexica and ontologies on the semantic web or only those resources represented in RDF) in Section 3. In Section 4 we use this model to investigate how best to exploit ontological information to represent cases of systematic polysemy while at the same time avoiding the problems raised by the sense enumeration lexicon model.

2 Ontology Modelling and Natural Language Meaning

If there were no real distinction to be made between ontological and semantic knowledge – or to be more accurate between how ontological and semantic knowledge is structured and arranged – it would be enough to link a lexical entry directly to an ontological vocabulary item. One could then use the inferential tools that have been developed for ontological representational languages like OWL to directly derive facts about, for example, synonymy and polysemy. It would then also be viable to treat a lexical resource like WordNet, which is essentially a semantic network hierarchically structured using lexical relations like hyponymy and meronymy, as an ontology (indeed WordNet has been used as an ontology in the past, although by now the limitations of such an approach have been made clear in works such as Gangemi et al. (2002) and Oltramari et al. (2002)). But there are in fact some important differences between the two types of resource. Clarification on the differences in the arrangement and design of lexica and ontologies comes in the form of recent normative work on ontology design and especially via ontology evaluation methodologies. One of the most influential of these methodologies is OntoClean(Guarino and Welty (2004)). OntoClean provides a series of clearly formulated guidelines and suggestions for designing and evaulating ontologies based on well-studied metaphysical principles relating to such (technical) properties as *identity*, *rigidity*, *unity* – all of which turn out to be extremely salient for evaluating ontology design decisions. What is important for our purposes here is that the OntoClean principles are somewhat independent of those considerations based purely on language use and native speaker intuition that play a central role in the standard lexical semantic definitions of relations like hyponymy and synonymy. On the other hand the kinds of semantic information one would want to represent in a lexicon will include not just descriptions of the types of thing that a word refers to in the world, i.e., the extensional aspect of a word's meaning, but also information about language use, e.g., data about how and in what contexts a word can refer to different things. In addition, the association between an ontological term and its label is of a different kind from the association of a word sense or a word meaning with its head form[1]. For a more general overview on the differences between lexica and ontology see Hirst's survey article, Hirst (2004).

These observations about the relative language independence of well designed ontologies are important in justifying the use of ontologies as resources that enable researchers interested in natural language semantics to not only compare the meanings of terms across languages, using the ontology like an *interlingua*, but also to study how linguistic concepts map onto a (relatively) language independent domain. The fact that the meanings of ontological items tend to be comparatively "stable" and that ontologies are usually represented in formal languages for which there exist automated inference engines makes them extremely valuable in this respect. How then do we use ontological information to represent and to reason about semantic information? As we mentioned above, given the differences between semantic and ontological information, it's probably best not to treat ontological vocabulary items as word senses and link lexical entries directly to ontological items. At the same time, we want to access the information stored in the ontology in order to describe and reason about semantic information, although in a restricted way. Below we will describe a model for the interaction between a lexicon and an ontology in the modelling of semantic information, and show how it can be applied by focusing on the representation of the semantic phenomena of polysemy.

3 A Model of the Lexicon-Ontology interface

In this section we give a brief sketch of the model, the Lexicon-Sense-Ontology model (LSO), that we will use in the rest of the paper for representing the lexico-ontology interface. LSO is based on the *lemon* model, but with a number of alterations, especially in terms of how LSO represents word meaning as distributed across the lexicon and the ontology: for us a sense is not necessarily always to be regarded as a reified pairing of a lexical entry with an ontological entity, as in *lemon*. In the LSO model a lexicon Lex in a language $\mathfrak{L}$ is represented as a finite set $\{l_1, ..., l_k\}$ of lexical entries each of which can be tagged with morphosyntactic information and each of which is associated with one or more sense objects that represent the meaning of the lexical entry[2]. The sense relation $sense \subseteq Lex \times Sense$ relates lexical entries together with their senses. In LSO *homophonous* words like *bank* and *bank* exist as separate entries and we make the assumption that all of the senses linked to a single lexical entry by $sense$ are somehow related or have some kind of overlap between them. An ontology is a logical theory $\mathcal{O}$ in a logical language $\mathcal{L}$ with vocabulary $\mathcal{V}$. Members of the set $Sense$ are linked to ontological vocabulary items that describe the references of these senses using the relation $hasRef \subseteq Sense \times \mathcal{V}$. By overloading this relation we define $hasRef \subseteq Lex \times \mathcal{V}$ to represent the case where a given lexical

[1]C.f for example the discussion in Pease and Li (2010) on the difference between SUMO term names and lexical entries.

[2]We view senses as abstract representations of the meaning of a lexical entry, so that together a lexical entry and a corresponding sense form a kind of "form-meaning [complex] with (relatively) stable and discrete semantic properties which stand in meaning relations such as antonymy and hyponymy" Cruse (1986).

entry has a sense with a certain extension represented by a ontological vocabulary item (this is useful when we don't want to explicitly mention sense objects, as in the formulae in Section 4.2). In addition the relation $hasRefSub \subseteq Lex \times \mathcal{V}$ is used in case a given lexical entry has a sense with a certain reference (which may or may not be explicitly enumerated as a vocabulary item) that if it were to be a vocabulary item would be subsumed by a named ontology vocabulary item. As we noted above we do not regard senses as reified pairings between lexical entries and ontological entities because we leave open the possibility that a sense may not be mapped to a concept in an ontology – or at least not via the $hasRef$ relation. In contrast to *lemon* we do not consider the semantics of lexical entries to exist only in the ontology, as per semantics by reference, but that to a large extent (language specific) semantic data is also represented in the sense layer (which is for us part of the lexicon) and especially in the interrelationships between the sense objects and in the relationships between the lexicon and ontology. It was for these reasons that we decided not to re-use the already existing *lemon* model in this work, but to develop a slightly different one – particularly since *lemon* has a clear formal semantics which strongly limits the kinds of interpretations that one can make. In the LSO model we have essentially three layers, a morpho-syntactic layer, a sense layer, and an ontological layer[3]. The sense layer is language specific since different languages will map their senses onto the ontology in distinct and incompatible ways[4].

4 Representing Polysemy

One of the main advantages of the LSO model is that it can help to avoid some of the many pitfalls associated with what Pustejovsky calls the Sense Enumeration Lexicon (SEL) (see Pustejovsky (1995)). The term SEL is used to describe any lexicon in which the related meanings of a lexical entry are represented as a set of different senses each of which is stored separately and without any kind of additional structure to relate the senses together. The problem with this sort of arrangement is that it makes it difficult to account for the creativity in natural languages that allows language users to regularly use words in novel ways and still be understood. Such a simplistic model also renders it impractical to represent the various different shades of meaning that any single word or lexical entry may potentially have; with SELs we lose out on the relatedness between the different senses of the same lexical item. For example, the English word *school* can mean both a building as well as an institution. These are two different senses of the same word, and they are clearly closely related, but what is the best way to represent this relation? One plausible answer, as suggested by Generative Lexicon (GL) theory (Pustejovsky (1995)) is that different kinds of common sense or ontological information are more accessible to the entries in a lexicon than others and that they license different type of sense extension. One general strategy, then, for avoiding SELs is to allow lexical entries to systematically pick out certain aspects of ontological knowledge via sense objects in a way that allows the easy generation of additional meanings based on a limited and finite *stored* set of senses for each lexical entry. In the following sections we show how to model this kind of lexicon-ontology interaction and also how to represent polysemy using LSO.

4.1 Dealing with Semi-productivity in Polysemy

An important issuse to take into consideration here is that polysemy tends to be semi-productive and so an impoverished sense layer or even the lack of one would over generate instances of polysemy. For instance in Parole Simple Clips, a large scale wide coverage Italian lexicon (Lenci et al. (2000)), a polysemy alternation is recorded for proper nouns referring to locations between the types `HUMAN-GROUP` and `GEOPOLITICALLOCATION`: so that the name of a location like *Genova* can also name the inhabitants, or a representative group of inhabitants, from that location. However this rule doesn't apply to imaginary locations like `Eldorado` that in other linguistic respects seem to behave just like real locations. The

[3]With the first two of these layers comprising the lexicon.

[4]To put it crudely this tripartite division reflects a kind of rough division of labour between those linguists who concern themseleves with morpho-syntactic data; those linguists who concern themselves mostly with the peculiarities of natural language semantics; and finally ontology engineers.

PLANT-FRUIT alternation is well known and exists in many languages. In some languages, however, it interacts with a derivation rule. So that for instance in Italian many plants have masculine names whereas the fruit is feminine[5]. In order to know when the regular polysemy is acting without change of morphological gender, we need to allow for a reasonably complex interaction between lexicon and ontology that depends on factors such as whether the plant is relatively small in size or whether the fruit and tree are "exotic" to Italy. We can then say that this alternation is in fact limited to a fairly large subset of fruit plants that can be identified productively by accessing ontological knowledge.[6]

4.2 Using Default Rules

Polysemy alternations tend to be reasonably regular but admit of exceptions (which differ across languages) that can usually be enumerated as finite lists of exceptions or described using simple logical formulae that refer to ontological vocabulary items. This would suggest the use of a non-monotonic logic to represent polysemy in terms of ontological knowledge, and indeed, as we shall see below Reiter's Default Logic (Reiter (1987)) lends itself particularly well to this task. One should bear in mind, however, that regardless of the exact representation framework that we use or how these rules are implemented in an actual application, what is important here is to emphasise the use of information about natural language semantics to constrain *how* we access the ontological layer so that any application that uses the ontological data doesn't overgenerate 'examples' of polysemy.

Default logic is a popular non-monotonic knowledge representation language that uses rules to represent facts and statements that hold by default in addition to knowledge bases consisting of sets of first order logic or description logic formulae. Default rules are usually represented in the form $\frac{\phi:\psi_1,\ldots,\psi_k}{\chi}$ – where the formula χ, the *consequent*, follows from ϕ, the *pre-requisite*, if it is consistent to assume $\psi_1, \ldots, \psi_k$, the *justifications*. In addition we can use classical rules to formulate the exceptions, that is, the cases when it's not acceptable to assume $\psi_1, \ldots, \psi_k$. A default theory is a pair consisting of a set of default rules, and a set of classical logic formulae. The semantics for default logic is usually given in terms of *extensions* which are sets of formulae with appropriate closure conditions that we won't describe here (Reiter (1987)). Default Logic is an appropriate formalism for cases where we are dealing with rules for which we do not know the set of exceptions beforehand or when it would be too difficult to enumerate or describe them all; the use of default logic also helps to emphasise that we are dealing with what is *usually* the case. So for example, take the ANIMAL-FOOD alternation, according to which the same word used to name an animal is also *usually* used to name the (edible) flesh of that animal. Say we are working with an English language lexicon and an ontology with the classes Animal and Edible, and the relation fleshOf, then given the lexical entry l, and ontology vocabulary items c, c', we can give the following default rule:

$$\frac{hasRef(l,c) \wedge c \sqsubseteq \texttt{Animal} \wedge \texttt{fleshOf}(c',c) \wedge c' \sqsubseteq \texttt{Edible} : hasRef(l,c')}{hasRef(l,c')}.$$

This rule is an example of a *normal default rule*, that is a rule where the justifications and the consequent are the same. We can read the rule above as saying that: if it is true that l can refer to the class c, a subclass of *Animal*, and if the flesh of the members of c, represented by the class c' is edible – then if it's consistent to assume that l has the extension c', we can indeed assume it to be the case. We can then add a (classical logic) rule such that lexical entries such as *Pig* and *Cow* do not name the (edible) flesh of the animals referred to by those nouns in English. So that if $l = Pig$, then it is not consistent to assume that l can also mean the flesh of a pig. In effect then, through the implementation of such default rules, we can use the ontological layer of a lexico-semantic resource modelled using the LSO model to justify polysemy alternations. In the example we gave above two things have the same name because one is a part of the other – and we can check using the ontology what this part_of relation actually consists in. This is why it's important to be able to make a clear distinction between what is in the ontology and

[5]For example, apple tree and apple are *melo* and *mela* respectively.

[6]See Copestake and Briscoe (1995) for an interesting discussion of the contextual blocking effects of both lexical and ontological knowledge on polysemy rules.

what is in the lexicon in order to avoid the danger of circularity in these explanations. The "messy" semantic details of how a language like English represents the relationship between animals and their flesh, the socio-cultural reasons as to why *Beef* or *Pork* are used instead of *Cow* and *Pig*, and that serve to somehow "distort" the ontological data, are part of the structure of the sense layer. It is especially important to emphasise this since there are languages such as West Greenlandic Eskimo in which the kind of "grinding" phenomena discussed above doesn't occur (Nunberg and Zaenen (1992)). The benefit of having a relation like $hasRefSub$ is that we don't need to explicitly store senses and this can be very useful. For example, according to OntoClean principles the class of Animals is not subsumed by the class of Physical Objects instead there exists a different (part_of) relation linking an animal with its physical body. But the large majority of languages do not seem to lexicalise this difference, and so the following rule can be justified for most lexica: given $l \in Lex, c \in \mathcal{V}$, then

$$hasRef(l, c) \wedge c \sqsubseteq \texttt{Animal} \rightarrow hasRefSub(l, \texttt{PhysicalObject}).$$

This ability to refer to senses without storing them at least partially obviates some of the problems inherent in SELs. It also means that we can distinguish cases when a sense really does have an existing ontology class as an extension (this is especially true in technical and scientific contexts or in controlled versions of natural languages); on the other hand it may be that the ontology we're using doesn't contain a specific concept, e.g., there may not be an ontology item corresponding to the fruit Persimmon, necessitating that the word sense in question be linked to the more general class `Fruit` using $hasRefSub$.

With this kind of semantic-ontological information available we can easily construct systems for word sense disambiguation that can capture cases of polysemy by keeping track of the kinds of ontological knowledge that lead to polysemy while at the same time avoiding overgeneration by storing exceptions to the rules. The problem is how to implement the default rules themselves. The idea of extending description logics with default rules hit a major stumble due to the undecidability result in Baader and Hollunder (1995) – although they did show that decidability was preserved in the case of formulae with named individuals. In certain limited cases, however, such as for example the extension of description logics with normal default rules using a special kind of default semantics, decidability is preserved, but further work needs to be done in order to study the extent to which this will enable us to capture the kinds of semantic information that we want to represent (see Sengupta et al. (2014)). There are also several other ways of integrating description logic databases with default rules: see for example the work of Dao-Tran et al. (2009) which makes use of conjunctive query programs. Further work in this area will look into the best combination of formalism and efficient knowledge representation tools in order to represent natural language semantics using the LSO model.

4.3 Further Observations on Polysemy and the Structuring of the Sense Layer

One issue that commonly arises when trying to model polysemy phenomena using ontologies concerns the need to have access to knowledge about what is *usually* the case in both the physical world and in social reality; and here one should stress the importance of ontologies that deal with social reality with respect to this task. Polysemy occurs in contexts where the association between two or more entities or aspects of the same entity is strong enough that the advantage gained by using the same term to refer to both of them outweighs whatever risk there may be of confusion[7]. In this section we look at how such ontological knowledge can be useful in interpreting polysemy. For instance one particularly interesting class of examples of polysemy is that relating to lexical entries that name both information objects and physical objects such as *book*, *play*, *poem*, and *film*. For instance take the lexical entry *book* that can mean both `BOOK_AS_PHYSICALOBJECT` and `BOOK_AS_INFORMATIONOBJECT` as in the sentences

- *The book had yellowed with age and gave off a musty odour* and
- *The book was thrilling and suspenseful.*

[7]Obviously the trade-off varies with context, so that referring to a customer as "the ham sandwich" is a viable communication strategy in a deli.

It is unlikely that the concept BOOK_AS_PHYSICALOBJECT will be explicitly modelled in most ontologies and so *hasRefSub* comes in useful again. The sense of *book* in which it refers to an information object seems to be primary here; books are informational objects that are *usually* instantiated as physical objects or are *usually* stored in some kind of physical format[8]. On the other hand lectures are not, or at least not by default, published but are instead more closely associated with events and informational objects.

- *?The lecture is lying on the table.*
- *The lecture is on my hard drive. / The lecture took an hour. / The lecture was both enthralling and informative.*

The first sentence in the preceding sounds slightly odd, but is still understandable since lectures are often instantiated as sets of notes or occasionally published as books (instead, a sentence like *The lecture notes are lying on the table* is much more acceptable); the second instance is much more acceptable because of the common practice of storing footage of lectures or the slides used in a lecture in a digital format; the final two are both completely acceptable. Other informational objects like conversations and speeches are not associated with any particular physical format by default, and can only in special contexts be considered as acceptable arguments with predicates that select for physical object arguments, although they are much more acceptable with predicates that select for digital or analogue data objects. Another important issue when dealing with polysemy is to determine when one sense of a polysemic word is somehow more primary or *established* to use Cruse's terminology in Cruse (1986); this in turn would suggest some further structuring in the sense layer to account for the distributions of senses. To take the example given in Cruse (1986):

- *I'm not interested in the cover design, or the binding – I'm interested in the novel.*
- *?I'm not interested in the plot, or the characterisation, or anything of that nature – I'm interested in the novel.*

This example is also productive in that it holds for films when stored in DVDs (e.g., *I'm not interested in the case design or the booklet – I'm interested in the movie.?I'm not interested in the plot, or the acting or anything like that – I'm interested in the movie.*).The established or primary status of certain senses of a word is useful information that can go in the sense layer since it does affect how a word behaves.

5 Conclusions and Further Work

Lexical semanticists have studied the lexicon-ontology interface for many years, investigating the best way to divide up semantic and ontological information at the level of theory. Nowadays, thanks in large part to the popularity of the linked data movement, we actually have the possibility of accessing large-scale wide-coverage ontologies that are comprehensive enough to study these more general theories of the lexicon using computers; at the same time ontology engineering is maturing as a discipline and has also been able to contribute a great deal to the debate in its own turn. In this article we have attempted to introduce a general framework to study some of these issues. What's clear however is that most existing ontologies are not designed according to the strict constraints described in the OntoClean model – and that many of them do in fact make the kinds of confusions between lexical and ontological information that we alluded to above. However we still feel that enough of a distinction is observed in practice to render our work useful in the context of lexicon-ontology interfacing, even if it's as an idealisation. We are currently in the process both of enriching our model in order to describe diverse types of semantic information and of determining how to actually implement some of the ideas introduced in this paper using currently available lexicons and ontologies. In future we plan to place a greater emphasis in our research on producing resources and tools, e.g., lexical databases that answer given queries either by searching among existing senses or by triggering the correct rules to produce senses on the fly.

[8]Once more Default Logic again seems to be the obvious choice to represent these kinds of facts.

References

Baader, F. and B. Hollunder (1995). Embedding defaults into terminological representation systems. *J. Automated Reasoning 14*, 149–180.

Cimiano, P., J. McCrae, P. Buitelaar, and E. Montiel-Ponsoda (2013). On the role of senses in the ontology-lexicon. In *New Trends of Research in Ontologies and Lexical Resources*, pp. 43–62. Springer.

Copestake, A. and T. Briscoe (1995). Semi-productive polysemy and sense extension. *Journal of semantics 12*(1), 15–67.

Cruse, D. (1986). *Lexical Semantics*. Cambridge, UK: Cambridge University Press.

Dao-Tran, M., T. Eiter, and T. Krennwallner (2009). Realizing default logic over description logic knowledge bases. In C. Sossai and G. Chemello (Eds.), *Symbolic and Quantitative Approaches to Reasoning with Uncertainty, 10th European Conference, ECSQARU 2009, Verona, Italy, July 1-3, 2009. Proceedings*, Volume 5590 of *Lecture Notes in Computer Science*, pp. 602–613. Springer.

Gangemi, A., N. Guarino, A. Oltramari, R. Oltramari, and S. Borgo (2002). Cleaning-up wordnet's top-level. In *In Proc. of the 1st International WordNet Conference*.

Guarino, N. and C. A. Welty (2004). An overview of ontoclean. See Staab and Studer (2004), pp. 151–172.

Hirst, G. (2004). Ontology and the lexicon. See Staab and Studer (2004), pp. 209–230.

Lenci, A., N. Bel, F. Busa, N. Calzolari, E. Gola, M. Monachini, A. Ogonowski, I. Peters, W. Peters, N. Ruimy, M. Villegas, and A. Zampolli (2000). SIMPLE: A General Framework for the Development of Multilingual Lexicons. *International Journal of Lexicography 13*(4), 249–263.

Mccrae, J., G. Aguado-De-Cea, P. Buitelaar, P. Cimiano, T. Declerck, A. Gómez-Pérez, J. Gracia, L. Hollink, E. Montiel-Ponsoda, D. Spohr, and T. Wunner (2012, December). Interchanging lexical resources on the semantic web. *Lang. Resour. Eval. 46*(4), 701–719.

Nunberg, G. and A. Zaenen (1992). Systematic polysemy in lexicology and lexicography. In *EURALEX'92. Papers submitted to the 5th EURALEX International Congress of Lexicography*.

Oltramari, A., A. Gangemi, N. Guarino, and C. Masolo (2002). Restructuring WordNet's Top-Level: The OntoClean approach. In *Proceedings of LREC2002 (OntoLex workshop). Las Palmas, Spain*.

Pease, A. and J. Li (2010). Controlled English to Logic Translation. In R. Poli, M. Healy, and A. Kameas (Eds.), *Theory and Applications of Ontology*. Springer.

Pustejovsky, J. (1995). *The Generative Lexicon*. Cambridge, MA: MIT Press.

Reiter, R. (1987). Readings in nonmonotonic reasoning. Chapter A Logic for Default Reasoning, pp. 68–93. San Francisco, CA, USA: Morgan Kaufmann Publishers Inc.

Sengupta, K., P. Hitzler, and K. Janowicz (2014). Revisiting default description logics and their role in aligning ontologies.

Staab, S. and R. Studer (Eds.) (2004). *Handbook on Ontologies*. International Handbooks on Information Systems. Springer.

Modelling time and space in Brazilian culture

Daniel Couto-Vale
RWTH Aachen
daniel.couto-vale@ifaar.rwth-aachen.de

Rodrigo de Oliveira
University of Aberdeen
rodrigodeoliveira@abdn.ac.uk

Abstract

In order to analyze and synthesize spatial language in Brazilian Portuguese automatically, a machine needs a linguistic model that fits the sort of wordings that adult Brazilians express and can understand. In this paper, we analyzed a corpus of spatial actions and relations manually using the categories of the Generalized Upper Model (GUM) and verified how far this linguistic model covered the instances of our corpus. We found uncovered spatial relations and contextualization constraints and, based on these findings, we proposed (a) a reformulation of GUM's typology for relational figures as well as (b) the notion of relational stability as a culture-specific contextualization constraint.

1 Introduction

Imagine you are in your flat sitting on an autonomous wheelchair, which you can control via voice commands. After someone knocks on the entrance door, you say to the wheelchair: "Take me to the door." The expected reply by the wheelchair would be: "OK. I'll take you there." Full understanding can only be established in such a way if the wheelchair is able to use context to infer which door you meant. Since the flat has many doors (e.g. to the toilet, living room, etc.) the nominal group "the door" represents the most relevant door in the context of situation. Likewise, the reply by the wheelchair omits the type of thing where it is taking you, and it is your job to understand that "there" refers to a position relative to the door. If we wish to allow humans to speak to machines like we do to other humans, we need to model what kinds of phenomena are represented by utterances first, before we can recognize the relevant ones in context.

Modeling the content of an utterance is the domain of semantics while relating this content to context of the utterance is the domain of pragmatics. Such a linguistic model can be reused across different contexts as it is meant to be used in the interface between semantics and pragmatics, i.e. before the contextualization step during understanding and after the sentence planning step during verbalization. Therefore it must make the minimum meaning commitment to avoid ambiguity in linguistic analysis, while being specific enough to specify a unique grammatical unit for linguistic synthesis.

One specific use of language is to describe the location of things; this manifestation of language has been labelled *spatial language*. In modelling spatial language, geometrical accounts have been the predominant first choice of researchers (Herskovits, 1980; Talmy, 1983; Kracht, 2002). The second choice has been to use relaxed geometrical rules (Talmy, 1983; Herskovits, 1985; Kracht, 2002; Francez and Steedman, 2006). However, Zwarts (2005) and Bateman (2010) show that language commits to qualitative and functional notions of space that are independent of time and three-dimensional regions. With a functional approach, the semantic contribution of spatial terms is formalized as an intermediary constraint for identifying entities and relations in a situation and not as a reference to pre-conceived entities and relations (Eschenbach, 1999).

Adopting a systemic functional approach, Matthiessen (1995, 1998) and Halliday and Matthiessen (1999, 2004, 2014) described the transitivity system of English in terms of participant and circumstance roles and Participant and Circumstance classes of semantic constituent. In order to treat spatial language, Bateman et al. (1995, 2010) defined the Element class of semantic constituents, which can be both a Thing and a Circumstance. This resulted in the Generalized Upper Model (GUM 3.0) and its spatial extension (GUM-space, Hois et al., 2009) [1], an ontology of semantic units following the principles of unique specification and minimum commitment.

However, being primarily designed after linguistic evidence in English and German, the question of to what extent GUM also applies for other natural languages, such as Brazilian Portuguese, remains partially unanswered. In this paper, we verify how far the model covers a Brazilian corpus of spatial actions and relations [2]. With our findings, we propose a reformulation of GUM's typology[3] for relational figures and conceptualize stability constraints for contextualization.

2 GUM Coverage

We collected a representative corpus of spatial relations and directed motions in Brazilian Portuguese from the tourist guide "Guia Essencial de Curitiba" (Essential Guide to Curitiba)[4]. Clauses and phrases were annotated with the terminology of GUM and GUM-space: the ones which were not predicted by the linguistic theory inside GUM were kept separate as a support for reviewing the model. After annotation, the instances of each class were inspected: when more specific linguistic variants were found under the same class, they were marked for the review phase.

Out of 304 instances of spatial figures (type of clause meaning) and spatial circumstances (type of phrase meaning), 288 (94.7%) were covered by GUM's terminology and 16 (5.3%) were not, including Examples 1-3:

(1) abrigava teatros e cafés
housed theaters and cafés
'[it] used to house theaters and cafés'

(2) o Palácio Avenida, sede do banco HSBC,
the Palace Avenida headquarters of-the bank HSBC
'the Avenida Palace, headquarters of HSBC,'

(3) o campanário da igreja com a bandeira do Brasil no topo
the bell-tower of-the church with the flag of-the Brazil at-the top
'the bell tower of the church with the Brazilian flag at its top'

Out of the covered instances, 51 (16.8%) were marked as underspecified, i.e. they are only spatial relations after contextualization (cf. Section 4), and 46 (15.1%) had an uncovered temporal variation, including the opposing pairs in Examples 4-5 and 6-7.

(4) ir para a praia
go to the beach
'going to the beach' (and staying there for a while)

(5) chegar até a Praça Espanha/Batel Soho
arrive until the square Espanha/Batel Soho
'to arrive at Espanha/Batel Soho Square' (no commitment to a longer stay)

(6) do outro lado da praça fica a entrada do Passeio Público
of-the other side of-the square is.STABLE the entrance of-the Passeio Público
'on the other side of the square is the entrance to Passeio Público'

[1] The ontology files can be downloaded at: http://www.ontospace.uni-bremen.de/ontology/gum.html

[2] Curitiba Corpus: https://docs.google.com/spreadsheet/ccc?key=0AjjU8ITs-OqudDE1MkZoS19IQWJ2Tks0NE5ONFhrZEE&usp=sharing

[3] https://github.com/DanielCoutoVale/UpperModel

[4] http://blogdapulp.wordpress.com/guias-de-viagem/guia-essencial-de-curitiba/

(7) em seu lugar estava a antiga Matriz
at its place was the old Matriz
'in its place used to be the old Matriz [church]'

2.1 Subjectless Clauses

It is worth noticing that the way Brazilian Portuguese anchors clauses to paragraph topics is different from that of English and German. While German and English always have a clausal subject related to the topic of the paragraph in the form of a noun-group, Brazilian Portuguese does not.

On the one hand, Brazilian Portuguese may conflate the subject with the finite process or auxiliary as in '**está** a três quadras da Alameda' (***it-is*** *three blocks away from Alameda*). This subject-finite conflation leaves a trace in the finite: for instance, if the subject were the speaker, the clause would be '**estou** a três quadras da Alameda' (***I-am*** *three blocks away from Alameda*).

On the other hand, Brazilian Portuguese also allows completely subject-less clauses such as 'são três quadras até a Alameda' (**are three blocks until Alameda*), whereby the thing which is three blocks away from the Alameda (the functional subject) leaves no trace in the clause structure because the finite process or auxiliary agrees with the direct complement. The semantics of subjectless clauses is not covered by GUM 3.0 and they account for 2 instances in the corpus.

3 Reviewing Spatial Relations

In order to extend GUM over uncovered phenomena, it was necessary to restructure the current typology of spatial relations. We remodelled the semantic constituents of spatial relations proposed by Bateman et al. (2010) by adding 4 new dimensions: *intensiveness*, *predication*, *version* and *stability*. In the remaining of this section we shall describe with examples from the corpus how this new structure of the ontology fits more accurately the flexibility of spatial language observed in Brazilian Portuguese.

3.1 Relational Intensiveness

Spatial relating figures may have two constitutional structures: the Intensive is composed by a process between two simple things, such as 'the frost covers the grass', and the Incidential is composed by a process, a spatial relative and a simple thing, such as 'the frost is on the grass'.

3.2 Relational Predication

Relating figures may have different participants as the subject. A relational predicate may receive either the domain as subject (domain-receptive) or the range as subject (range-receptive).

For Intensive relating figures, Portuguese offers two predicate options: a domain-receptive predicate as in 'a geada cobre o gramado' (*the frost covers the grass*, Figure 1(a)) and a range-receptive one by reordering the constituents and inserting the auxiliary 'ser' and the case 'por' as in 'o gramado **é** coberto **pel**a geada' (*the grass* ***is*** *covered* ***by*** *the frost*, Figure 1(b)).

And for Extensive relating figures, Portuguese constructs the relational voice by varying the type of the relative constituent. The relative of the domain-receptive voice is a Circumstance composed by a relation and a relatum as in 'a geada fica em cima do gramado' (*the frost is on the grass*, cf. Figure 2(a)) and that of the range-receptive voice is a SetUp composed by a relator and a relation as in 'a grama fica com a geada em cima' (*the grass has the frost on it*, cf. Figure 2(b)).

3.3 Relational Version

Known in linguistics as diathesis, another variation found in the corpus lies in the different mappings of logical roles (such as locatum or locator) to the relational roles (domain, range, *relator*, and *relatum*). We could cover all relating figures with two mappings and four diathetic roles.

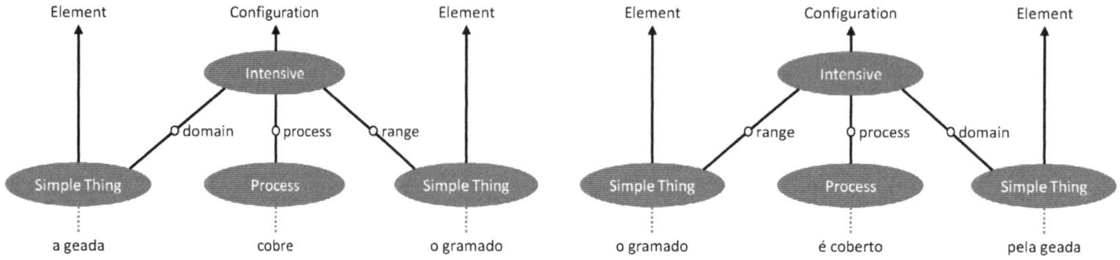

(a) domain-receptive Intensive. (b) range-receptive Intensive.

Figure 1: Intensive Relating figures.

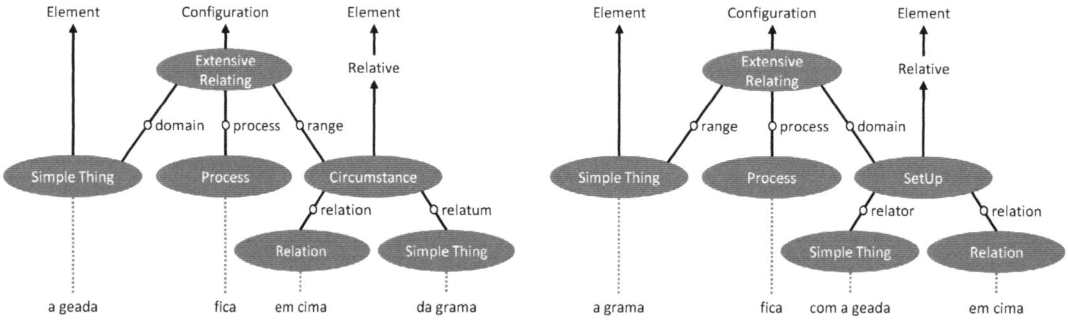

(a) domain-receptive Extensive. (b) range-receptive Extensive.

Figure 2: Extensive Relating figures.

On the one hand, the Featuring mapping makes a *carrier* out of domains and relators and a *feature* out of ranges and relata as in 'o palácio abriga a prefeitura' (*the palace houses the prefecture*, Figure 3(a)) and 'o palácio é sede da prefeitura' (*the palace is headquarters of the prefecture* 3(b)).

On the other hand, the Marking mapping makes a *mark* out of domains and relators and a *setting* out of ranges and relata as in 'a prefeitura habita o palácio' (*the prefecture inhabits the palace*, Figure 3(c)) and 'a prefeitura fica dentro do palácio' (*the prefecture is inside the palace*, Figure 3(d)).

For this reason, in the diathesis of spatial roles, the locatum role filled by 'a prefeitura' (*the prefecture*) specifies both *feature* and *mark* roles and the locator role filled by 'o palácio' (*the palace*) specifies both *carrier* and *setting* roles.

In the phrase level as qualifiers, intensiveness, voice, and version are also present. Intensive relations make domain-receptive voice with the present participle form of the process as in 'abrigando a prefeitura' (housing the prefecture) and range-receptive voice with the past participle form as in 'abrigada pelo palácio' (housed by the palace), while Incidential relations make domain-receptive voice with a *Circumstance* 'sede da prefeitura' (headquarters of the prefecture) and range-receptive with a *SetUp* with 'com' as in 'com o palácio de sede' (with the palace as headquarters), thereby leaving the process undefined, i.e. without any lexical material.

3.4 Stability of Relation and of Action Result

Using image schemas, (Araújo, 2008) made an analysis of spoken-language expression pairs such as 'eles estão **no** Maranhão' (*they are **at** Maranhão [but a more precise nature of this relation is not provided]*) and 'eles estão **pro** Maranhão' (*they are **at** Maranhão [but their relation to the State of Maranhão is less stable than their relation to another state]*). Such linguistic evidence shows that relational stability plays a fundamental role in specifying which kind of spatial relation is being referred to, that is, stay or residence in a Federative State. And this variation is grammaticalized as a specification of spatial

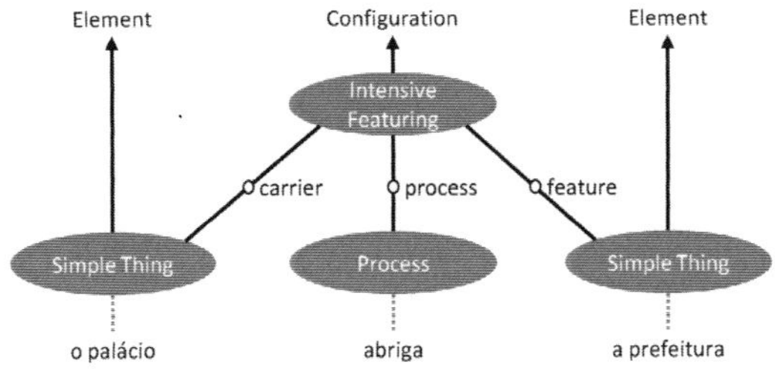

(a) Intensive and Featuring (Housing).

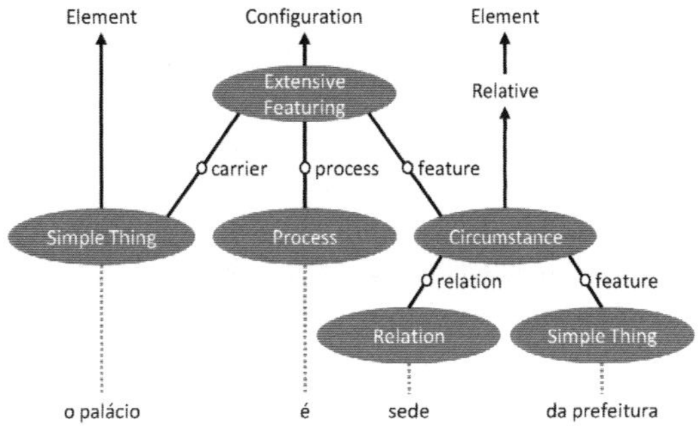

(b) Extensive and Featuring (Disposition).

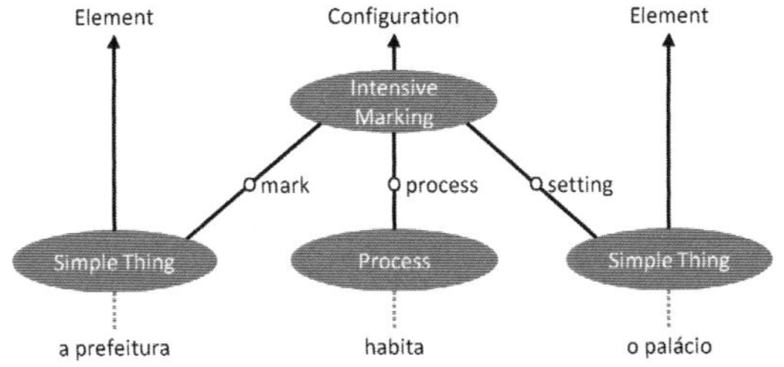

(c) Intensive and Marking (Habitation).

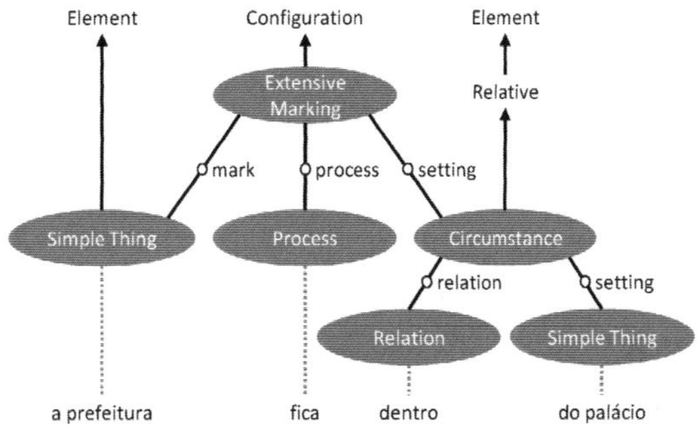

(d) Extensive and Marking (Locating).

Figure 3: Featuring and Marking figures.

modality.

The same phenomenon was observable in our corpus in directed motion results. While processes such as **ir** (*go*) and **vir** (*come*) are used both for traveling and migratory movements, the spatiotemporal modality is differentiated: migratory movements take the spatial modality term **para** (*to.stable*) and traveling ones take **até** (*to*) as in 'vieram **para** a cidade' (*they migrated here to the city*) and 'vieram **até** a cidade' (*they traveled here to the city*). This means that migrants and turists share the same process of directed motion in Brazil while the kind of the changed relation between them and cities (stay or residence) is constrained by the stability contrast between the spatial modality terms **para** and **até**. This stability opposition is by no means attached exclusively to traveling and migratory movements as they also allow the contrast between 'ir **para** a praia' (*go to the beach [and stay there]*) and 'ir **até** a praça' (*go to the square [and possibly move on]*).

For Extensive spatial relations, stability was marked in our corpus by process alternation. In domain-receptive voice, the process **ficar** (*relate.stable*) specified the stability of the relation while the process **estar** (*relate*) made no stability commitments. In range-receptive voice, the process **ficar** ***com*** (*be-related.stable*) specifies stability and **ter** (*be-related*) makes no stability commitments. Outside our corpus, instability commitments are also to be found. The choice of the static spatial modality term **para** (*at.instable*) instead of **em** (*at*) as in 'eles estão pro Maranhão' (*they are [currently] at Maranhão*) in the spoken language corpus of Araújo (2008) specifies instability in domain-receptive voice.

4 Cultural Commitments

Our corpus shows that Brazilian Portuguese very often construes spatial relations of unspecific kind that need to be contextually understood as containment, accessibility, distance, projection or something else. In contrast, specification occurs in four other dimensions: intensiveness, voice, version, stability.

In Brazil, the type of relation is inferred from the kind of entities and the stability of the relation between them. This would justify the oppositions between 'vir para a cidade' (migrate to the city) / 'vir até a cidade (travel to the city) and 'ir para a praia' (go lay on the beach) / 'ir até a praia' (go up to the beach), in which the relational stability is used as a constraint for contextualizing the kind of relation between the person and the city or between the person and the beach.

Stability and type of entities stand for relation types not only in our corpus but also in the Brazilian culture and legislation, in which the recognition of several kinds of relations[5] are based on stability. These linguistic phenomena were not predicted by GUM 3.0, which is due to the fact that the model was created using corpora of German and English. When facing different languages, not only linguistic variation is under scrutiny, but also other underlying social phenomena.

5 Conclusion

In this paper, we have shown that Brazilian Portuguese construes space with a four-dimensional variation in intensiveness, voice, version, and stability. Supported by this linguistic evidence, we have proposed a reviewed typology of relating figure to be included in the Generalized Upper Model (GUM) and culture-specific additions such as stability to be included in a GUM extension named GUM-Brazil. With this change, we make the linguistic model fit Brazilian Portuguese flexibility more accurately and avoid supposed issues of extreme underspecification (or meaninglessness) which are barriers for applied linguistics and for the automation of linguistic analysis and synthesis in general.

References

Araújo, P. J. P. (2008). Aspectos semântico-cognitivos de usos especiais das preposições para e em na fala de comunidades quilombolas. Master's thesis, Universidade de São Paulo.

Bateman, J. A. (2010, August). Situating spatial language and the role of ontology: Issues and outlook. *Language and Linguistics Compass 4*(8), 639–664.

Bateman, J. A., R. Henschel, and F. Rinaldi (1995). The Generalized Upper Model 2.0. In *Proceedings of the ECAI94 Workshop: Comparison of Implemented Ontologies.*

Bateman, J. A., J. Hois, R. Ross, and T. Tenbrink (2010). A linguistic ontology of space for natural language processing. *Artificial Intelligence 174*(14), 1027–1071.

Eschenbach, C. (1999). Geometric structures of frames of reference and natural language semantics. *Spatial Cognition and Computation 1*(4), 329–348.

Francez, N. and M. Steedman (2006). Categorial grammar and the semantics of contextual prepositional phrases. *Linguistics and Philosophy 29*(4), 381–417.

Halliday, M. A. K. and C. M. Matthiessen (1999). *Construing experience through meaning: a language-based approach to cognition.* London/New York: Continuum.

Halliday, M. A. K. and C. M. Matthiessen (2004). *An Introduction to Functional Grammar.* New York: Oxford University Press.

Halliday, M. A. K. and C. M. Matthiessen (2014). *Halliday's introduction to functional grammar.* Routledge.

Herskovits, A. (1980). On the spatial uses of prepositions. In *Proceedings of the 18th Annual Meeting on Association for Computational Linguistics ACL 80*, pp. 1–5.

[5]Employment: Decreto-Lei n.5452/43, Art. 3o; Marriage: CR/88, Art. 226, §3o c/c CC, Art. 1.723, caput; Land ownership: CR/88, Art.183; Nationality: CR/88, Art. 12.

Herskovits, A. (1985). Semantics and pragmatics of locative expressions. *Cognitive Science* 9(3), 341–378.

Hois, J., T. Tenbrink, R. Ross, and J. A. Bateman (2009). Gum-space. The Generalized Upper Model spatial extension: A linguistically-motivated ontology for the semantics of spatial language. Technical report, Collaborative Research Center for Spatial Cognition, University of Bremen, SFB/TR8 Spatial Cognition.

Kracht, M. (2002). On the semantics of locatives. *Linguistics and Philosophy* 25(2), 157–232.

Matthiessen, C. M. (1995). *Lexicogrammatical cartography: English systems.* International Language Science.

Matthiessen, C. M. I. M. (1998). The TRANSITIVITY of space in topographic procedures. MS.

Talmy, L. (1983). How language structures space. In H. L. Pick and L. P. Acredolo (Eds.), *Spatial Orientation: Theory, Research, and Application*, pp. 225–282. New York: Plenum Press.

Zwarts, J. (2005). Prepositional aspect and the algebra of paths. *Linguistics and Philosophy* 28(6), 739–779.

Trimming a consistent OWL knowledge base, relying on linguistic evidence

Julien Corman
IRIT - Toulouse
julien.corman@irit.fr

Nathalie Aussenac-Gilles
IRIT, CNRS - Toulouse
aussenac@irit.fr

Laure Vieu
IRIT, CNRS - Toulouse
LOA - Trento
vieu@irit.fr

Abstract

Intuitively absurd but logically consistent sets of statements are common in publicly available OWL datasets. This article proposes an original and fully automated method to point at erroneous axioms in a consistent OWL knowledge base, by weakening it in order to improve its compliance with linguistic evidence gathered from natural language texts. A score for evaluating the compliance of subbases of the input knowledge base is proposed, as well as a trimming algorithm to discard potentially erroneous axioms. The whole approach is evaluated on two real datasets, with automatically retrieved web pages as a linguistic input.

Introduction

As they grow in size, knowledge bases (KBs) tend to contain statements which may make sense individually but, when taken together, violate common sense intuitions. As an illustration, consider the following set Ω of Description Logics (DL) formulas, issued from DBpedia (Mendes et al., 2012) :

Ex 1. $\Omega = \{$
(1) owningCompany(*Smithsonian Networks*, *Smithsonian Institution*),
(2) doctoralAdvisor(*Thaddeus S.C. Lowe*, *Smithsonian Institution*),
(3) doctoralAdvisor(*Nick Katz*, *Bernard Dwork*),
(4) $\top \sqsubseteq \forall$doctoralAdvisor.Person,
(5) $\top \sqsubseteq \forall$owningCompany.Company $\}$

From (1), (2), (4) and (5), the individual *Smithsonian Institution* must be an instance of both Company and Person, which may seem counterintuitive, and indeed does not correspond to the overall understanding of these two concepts within DBpedia. This kind of issue is common among OWL datasets, which should not be a surprise. The most conventional way of spotting this kind of errors in OWL is by checking consistency or coherence[1] of the input KB, but negation (or cardinality restriction) is underused in practice. As an illustration, according to the LODstats survey tool (Auer et al., 2012), which provides statistics about a sample of the Linked Open Data (LOD) cloud, the two most standard OWL constructs expressing negation, namely owl:disjointWith and owl:complementOf, have been observed 333 times and twice respectively, against more that 89 000 occurrences for owl:subClassOf.

Let us assume that Ω is part of a larger KB K, for instance a subset of DBpedia extracted for a specific application, or a set of OWL statements aggregated from multiple sources. Assume also that there are several other instances of Person and Company according to K and, to keep the example simple, that *Smithsonian Institution*, *Bernard Dwork*, doctoralAdvisor, and owningCompany do not appear in $K \setminus \Omega$. If most instances of Person and Company according to K are respectively human beings and companies, one can expect the term "the Smithsonian Institution" to appear with linguistic contexts which tend to characterize terms denoting other instances of Company according to K (e.g.

[1] in the DL sense, i.e. the satisfiability of all atomic concepts

the context "*X* was established"), but not other instances of `Person` (like "*X* was born in"). Similarly, "Bernard Dwork" should appear with contexts which are characteristic of terms denoting other instances of `Person` according to K. In other words, by checking the overall compliance of K with some linguistic input, it should be possible to identify some undesirable (`Person`(*Smithsonian Institution*)) and desirable (`Company`(*Smithsonian Institution*), `Person`(*Bernard Dwork*)) consequences of it.

The next problem consists in determining how K can be weakened in order to discard the former, but keep the latter. Even if one focuses here (for readability) on weakening Ω only, there are several options available. The view adopted here, which is also the most common in the knowledge base debugging literature, is that some axiom(s) of Ω should be discarded, but none of them unnecessarily. Then the only solution in this example consists in discarding (2).

The article investigates the applicability of such a trimming mechanism to moderately large input KBs (up to a few thousand statements), using automatically gathered web pages or snippets as linguistic input. To our knowledge, this is the first attempt to use linguistic evidence in order to automatically weaken an existing KB instead of extending it.

Section 1 reviews existing works in two closely related fields, KB extraction from texts and KB debugging, whereas section 2 introduces some conventions. Section 3 defines a score which evaluates the compliance with the linguistic data of any subbase of the input KB. Section 4 proposes an algorithm to trim the input KB based on this score. Section 5 evaluates the approach with two datasets.

1 State of the art

Knowledge base extraction from texts, or ontology learning (Cimiano, 2006; Buitelaar et al., 2005) aims at automatically building or enriching a knowledge base out of linguistic evidence. The work presented here borrows from a subtask named ontology population (which itself borrows from named entity classification), but only when the individuals and concepts of interest are known in advance (Cimiano and Völker, 2005; Tanev and Magnini, 2008; Giuliano and Gliozzo, 2008), which is a non-standard case, whereas ontology population generally considers retrieving new individuals likely to instantiate a given set of concepts. The objective differs also fundamentally from the one pursued in knowledge base extraction, in that the desired output of the process is a weaker KB from which potentially faulty statements have been discarded, not a stronger one. In that sense, this work pertains to knowledge base debugging, for which different tools or algorithms have been devised in the recent years, performing for instance a series of syntactic verifications (Poveda-Villalón et al., 2012), or submitting models (Ferré and Rudolph, 2012; Benevides et al., 2010) or consequences (Pammer, 2010) of the input KB to the user.

In a more automated fashion, diagnosis for Description Logics (Ribeiro and Wassermann, 2009; Schlobach, 2005; Friedrich and Shchekotykhin, 2005; Kalyanpur et al., 2006; Qi et al., 2008) deals with automated weakening of an input KB. An important difference though between this work and approaches based on diagnosis is that the latter assume that the input KB is inconsistent (or incoherent in the DL sense), or at least that some undesired consequences of K have been previously identified. Another drawback of KB diagnosis without an external source of knowledge (like the linguistic input used here) is the sheer number of candidate subbases, as experienced by (Schlobach, 2005).

2 Conventions

The reader is assumed familiar with the syntax and standard model-theoretic semantic of Description Logics (Baader, 2003). A *knowledge base* (KB) Γ is just a finite set of DL formulas. Following the usage in the DL community, the term *axiom* designates a formula $\phi \in \Gamma$, whereas a *consequence* ψ is a formula verified by all models of Γ. A KB is said consistent iff it admits a model. A DL *atomic concept* designates a unary predicate without logical connective or quantifier, like `Company` or `Person`, as opposed to a *complex concept*, like $\exists$`doctoralAdvisor`.$\neg$`Person`. A DL *role* is a binary predicate.

The method introduced here can in theory be applied to any KB in a DL with available reasoning facilities, in particular the DLs underlying the OWL DL and OWL 2 recommendations, but it is arguably better-suited for KBs in less expressive DLs, which also constitute the vast majority of the data available on the LOD cloud. Another requirement is the presence of linguistic terms denoting named individuals of the input KB, prototypically given by their OWL labels.

3 Compliance of a set of statements with a linguistic input

This section defines a score which reflects the compliance of a set of statements Γ with a linguistic corpus, and will be used in the next section to identify potentially faulty axioms in an input KB K. More precisely, what this score evaluates is the compliance with the linguistic input of the set $\sigma(\Gamma)$ of all consequences of Γ of the form $A(e)$ or $\neg A(e)$, where A and e are respectively a DL atomic concept and a DL individual, and such that there is at least one (other) instance e' of A according to Γ. For an atomic DL concept A, let $\sigma_A(\Gamma) \subseteq \sigma(\Gamma)$ denote the consequences of Γ of the form $A(e)$. Roughly speaking, for each $\psi = A(e)$ or $\psi = \neg A(e)$ in $\sigma(\Gamma)$, the method exploits linguistic contexts which, according to Γ, are characteristic of instances of A, based on $\sigma_A(\Gamma) \setminus \{e\}$, yielding a score $sc_\Gamma(\psi)$ for ψ. This score reflects how much the linguistic behavior of e resembles or deviates from the linguistic behavior of (other) instances of A. For instance, in example 1, let $\psi = \texttt{Person}(\textit{Smithsonian Institution})$, and assume that Ω is part of a larger (consistent) KB K. Then $\psi \in \sigma_{\texttt{Person}}(K) \subseteq \sigma(K)$, and the score $sc_K(\psi)$ of ψ is determined by the linguistic contexts shared by the individual *Smithsonian Institution* and other instances of `Person` according to K.

A first important observation is that no assumption is made regarding the veracity of a consequence like $\psi = \texttt{Person}(\textit{Smithsonian Institution})$. This would require some external knowledge about reality, which is beyond the scope of this work. The only source of knowledge is the input KB itself, paired with the linguistic input. For instance, the concept `Person` in K may encompass juridical persons, in which case one should expect the score $\text{sc}_K(\psi)$ to be high.

Another remark is that the linguistic term "person" does not play any function here. The label of the atomic concept `Person` could actually be "B_27", with no incidence on $sc_K(\psi)$. This contrasts with a relatively widespread approach in the knowledge base extraction literature, which consists in looking for (possibly learned) cooccurrence patterns (Hearst, 1992) between terms denoting instances and classes. For instance, if X denotes an individual and Y a concept, then the linguistic patterns "X is a Y" or "X and other Ys" tend to indicate that X is indeed an instance of Y. There are at least two reasons to prefer similarity of contexts to cooccurrences patterns for the precise task addressed here. First, when the instances and classes of interest are known in advance (which is the case here, but usually not for knowledge base extraction), similarity of contexts has been empirically shown to outperform cooccurrence patterns (Tanev and Magnini, 2008). This may be explained by the fact that retrieving a sufficient number of cooccurrences of a given pair of terms (e.g. "Thaddeus S.C. Lowe" and "person") is not always possible, whereas retrieving simple occurrences of a term (e.g. "Thaddeus S.C. Lowe") is obviously easier. Cooccurrences can also be harder to retrieve for more abstract concepts. For instance, "Virgin Holydays is [...] company", or "Virgin Holydays and other companies" both sound plausible, but "Virgin Holydays is [...] organization" or "Virgin Holydays and other organizations" is less likely to be found. The second reason is that terms denoting classes (prototypically common nouns) are arguably more ambiguous than terms denoting individuals (prototypically named entities). This does not completely solve the ambiguity issue though, in particular for homonyms (for instance, the term "JKF" may designate either a politician or an airport), and additional precautions may be taken for these, like the ones described in section 5.

Here is now a concrete proposition for the computation of $sc_\Gamma(\psi)$, given a consistent KB Γ and a consequence $\psi \in \sigma(\Gamma)$. The corpus is constituted of either web pages or snippets retrieved with a search engine, using as queries named entities which denote individuals appearing in Γ, generally given as OWL labels. A linguistic context in this setting is just an n-gram ($2 \leq n \leq 5$) immediately following or preceding a term of interest, and without punctuation mark. Borrowing from (Giuliano and Gliozzo, 2008), the observed frequencies of an n-gram s are adjusted based on the self information $\textit{self}(s)$, given by *self*$(s) = -\log p(s)$, the probability $p(s)$ being estimated with the Google Web 1T 5-gram corpus[2][3] (this intuitively penalizes n-grams with a high Google n-gram frequency).

Let *Cont* be the set of all contexts observed with individuals of Γ, and, if y is an individual, let $\mathbf{y} \in \mathbb{R}^{|Cont|}$ denote the vector of frequencies of contexts observed with y. The confidence score $\mathrm{sc}_\Gamma(\psi)$ is given either by :

Definition 3.1. $\mathrm{sc}_\Gamma(A(e)) = p(\Gamma \models A(x) \mid \mathbf{x} = \mathbf{e})$

Definition 3.2. $\mathrm{sc}_\Gamma(\neg A(e)) = 1 - p(\Gamma \models A(x) \mid \mathbf{x} = \mathbf{e})$

Intuitively, $p(\Gamma \models A(x) \mid \mathbf{x} = \mathbf{e})$ denotes the probability, for a random individual x with the same context frequency vector as e, that $\Gamma \models A(x)$. Applying Bayes' rule, it is equivalent to :

$$p(\mathbf{x} = \mathbf{e} \mid \Gamma \models A(x)) \cdot \frac{p(\Gamma \models A(x))}{p(\mathbf{x} = \mathbf{e})}$$

Let $\mathrm{inst}(\Gamma, C)$ denote the instances of concept C according to Γ, and $\sum \mathbf{y}$ the cumulated values of vector $\mathbf{y}$. Then $p(\Gamma \models A(x))$ can be estimated by $\frac{\sum_{x \in \mathrm{inst}(\Gamma, A)} \sum \mathbf{x}}{\sum_{x' \in \mathrm{inst}(\Gamma, \top)} \sum \mathbf{x}'}$.

Estimating $p(\mathbf{x} = \mathbf{e} \mid \Gamma \models A(x))$ is slightly more complex. Let $\cos(\mathbf{y}, \mathbf{y}')$ designate the cosine similarity between vectors $\mathbf{y}$ and $\mathbf{y}'$. If $X_{\mathbf{y}}^{\mathbf{y}'}$ is a random variable for $\cos(\mathbf{y}, \mathbf{y}')$, then $p(X_{\mathbf{y}}^{\mathbf{y}'} \leq \cos(\mathbf{y}, \mathbf{y}'))$ indicates how unexpectedly similar the observed linguistic behaviors of individuals y and y' are. Then $p(\mathbf{x} = \mathbf{e} \mid \Gamma \models A(x))$ can be estimated by $\sum_{e' \in \mathrm{inst}(\Gamma, A) \setminus \{e\}} \frac{p(X_{\mathbf{e}}^{\mathbf{e}'} \leq \cos(\mathbf{e}, \mathbf{e}'))}{|\mathrm{inst}(\Gamma, A) \setminus \{e\}|}$.

And similarly, $p(\mathbf{x} = \mathbf{e})$ can be estimated by $\sum_{e' \in \mathrm{inst}(\Gamma, \top) \setminus \{e\}} \frac{p(X_{\mathbf{e}}^{\mathbf{e}'} \leq \cos(\mathbf{e}, \mathbf{e}'))}{|\mathrm{inst}(\Gamma, \top) \setminus \{e\}|}$.

For the experiments described in section 5, $p(X_{\mathbf{e}}^{\mathbf{e}'} \leq \cos(\mathbf{e}, \mathbf{e}'))$ was computed by assuming a normal distribution of $X_{\mathbf{e}}^{\mathbf{e}'}$, whose parameters were estimated by maximum likelihood out of all pairwise cosine distances between individuals appearing in $\sigma(\Gamma)$.

The linguistic compliance score $\mathrm{sc}(\Gamma)$ for a set Γ of DL statements can then be defined as the mean of the scores of all $\psi \in \sigma(\Gamma)$:

Definition 3.3. $\mathrm{sc}(\Gamma) = \sum_{\psi \in \sigma(\Gamma)} \frac{\mathrm{sc}_\Gamma(\psi)}{|\sigma(\Gamma)|}$

4 Trimming a KB using linguistic compliance

This section shows how the compliance score which has just been defined can be used to refine an input KB K, in order to rule out potentially faulty axioms. Ideally, one would like to identify the subbases of K which are maximal wrt to set inclusion among the ones having a maximal compliance score. But in practice, even if this does not affect the worst-case complexity of the whole trimming process (dominated by the computation of $\sigma(K)$), the size of the search space (2^K) makes the identification of the optimal subbase(s) of K hardly feasible for realistically sized datasets. This is why the heuristic described by algorithm 1 was used for the experiments of section 5.

Intuitively, it consists in incrementally discarding the axiom which penalizes the most the linguistic compliance of the current base Γ, initialized with K. In other words, the selected axiom is the one which, if discarded, yields the immediate subbase with maximal compliance score. The output is a list containing successively discarded axioms, the first discarded ones being considered as the least reliable. The number n of axioms to discard is chosen as a parameter. Two limit cases are ignored for the sake of readability. First, it is assumed that $|\operatorname{argmax}_{\phi \in \Gamma} \mathrm{sc}(\Gamma \setminus \{\phi\})| = 1$, i.e. that there is a single least reliable

[2]https://catalog.ldc.upenn.edu/LDC2006T13

[3]Thanks to the linguistic department of the Erlangen-Nüremberg University for allowing us to query this corpus.

axiom at each iteration, which is usually the case if n is relatively small. Otherwise, the procedure can be adapted in a straightforward manner to return a set of lists of axioms, instead of a single list. The other (unlikely) limit case occurs when $\max_{\phi \in \Gamma} \text{sc}(\Gamma \setminus \{\phi\}) \leq \text{sc}(\Gamma)$, i.e. when no immediate subbase of Γ has a better compliance score than Γ. If this happens, the procedure should simply be interrupted, returning only the axioms discarded thus far.

Algorithm 1 Trimming heuristic

1: *OutputList* $\leftarrow$ *EmptyList* ;
2: $\Gamma \leftarrow K$;
3: **while** $|\Gamma| > |K| - n$ **do**
4:     *Ax* $\leftarrow \operatorname{argmax}_{\phi \in \Gamma} \text{sc}(\Gamma \setminus \{\phi\})$;
5:     *append(OutputList, Ax)* ;
6:     $\Gamma \leftarrow \Gamma \setminus \{\phi\}$;
7: **end while**

This procedure is only a heuristic, in that there is no guarantee that the complement in K of the n discarded axioms has an optimal compliance score among subbases of K (not even among subbases of K with cardinality $\geq |K| - n$).

An alternative approach was also experimented, which captures a slightly different intuition, namely that the loss of consequences of $\sigma(\Gamma)$ with low scores should be prioritized when selecting the axiom *Ax* to discard, line 4. Let $f(\phi) \in \mathbb{R}^*$ be the ordered list of all $\text{sc}_\Gamma(\psi)$ for $\psi \in \sigma(\Gamma \setminus \{\phi\})$. Then if $\preceq_l$ is the standard lexicographic order over $\mathbb{R}^*$, the axiom ϕ is discarded iff $\forall \phi' \in \Gamma \setminus \{\phi\} : f(\phi) \prec_l f(\phi')$.

5 Evaluation

Both approaches were evaluated with 2 consistent datasets, using a distinct evaluation protocol for each dataset. The first dataset is an automatically retrieved subset of DBpedia, thematically focused on tourism. It counts 5721 logical axioms, and 1095 DL named individuals, with relatively simple formulas (the least expressive underlying DL is $\mathcal{AL}^{(D)}$). This is an example of a lightweight KB, with a large predominance of ABox axioms (5336 over 5721). Additionally, it is a fragment of a large dataset (DBpedia) mainly built out of semi-structured data (Wikipedia infoboxes), but also partly issued from a collaborative effort (the DBpedia ontology), and therefore it is likely to contain nonsensical sets of statements. The procedure applied to obtain this KB is described in (Corman et al., 2015). In particular, individuals with potential homonyms (like *JFK*) have been discarded based on the existence of a Wikipedia disambiguation page, of other named individuals sharing their label in DBpedia, or simply if the number of matched web pages for (one of) the label(s) of the individual was too high. The corpus for this dataset was composed of approximately 60000 web pages retrieved with a search engine, using named individual labels as queries. The evaluation consisted in manually verifying whether a discarded axiom ϕ was actually erroneous, i.e. whether the understanding of some element of the signature of ϕ (named individual, atomic concept or role) was incompatible with its overall understanding within K.

The results of this first evaluation are presented in table 1. Columns "5", "10" and "20" give the number ("val.") and proportion ("prec.", for precision) of axioms manually identified as actually erroneous among the 5, 10 and 20 first discarded ones. Column "Ordering" specifies the method applied to select the discarded axiom ϕ at each iteration of the loop in algorithm 1 : "$\text{sc}(\Gamma \setminus \{\phi\})$" if $\phi = \operatorname{argmax}_{\phi \in \Gamma} \text{sc}(\Gamma \setminus \{\phi\})$, and "$\preceq_l$" if ϕ is obtained with the alternative approach (the lexicographic order) presented in section 4. The values obtained are encouraging, in that one can reasonably expect the proportion of erroneous within the whole KB to be much lower than the precision scores obtained here. A more thorough examination of the linguistic contexts responsible for these good results is still required though.

Ordering	5		10		20	
	val.	prec.	val.	prec.	val.	prec.
$\mathrm{sc}(\Gamma \setminus \{\phi\})$	3	0.6	3	0.3	9	0.45
$\preceq_l$	2	0.4	4	0.4	8	0.4

Table 1: Actually erroneous axioms among the first 5, 10 and 20 discarded ones for the DBpedia subset

Ordering	5		10		20	
	val.	prec.	val.	prec.	val.	prec./rec.
$\mathrm{sc}(\Gamma \setminus \{\phi\})$	5	1	6	0.6	9	0.45
$\preceq_l$	3	0.6	7	0.7	11	0.55

Table 2: Random axioms among the first 5, 10 and 20 discarded ones for the fragment of the fisheries ontology

The second dataset is a small randomly extracted fragment of the fisheries KB built for the NEON project,[4] which contains 169 logical axioms, involving only 20 named individuals (mostly geographical or administrative entities), with a more complex TBox (the least expressive underlying DL is $\mathcal{SI}$). This KB is arguably more reliable too, which allowed the experimentation of a more objective form of evaluation. It consists in artificially extending K with randomly generated axioms, before trying to discard them by application of the trimming algorithm. The assumption is that a randomly generated axiom is usually less reliable than a manually crafted one. The axiom generation procedure randomly selects an axiom $\phi \in K$, and yields an axiom ϕ' with the same syntactic structure, but in which all individuals, atomic concepts and roles have been randomly replaced by individuals, atomic concepts and roles appearing in K. For instance, if $\phi = A \sqsubseteq \forall r.\neg B$, then $\phi' = C \sqsubseteq \forall s.\neg D$, with C and D (resp. s) randomly chosen among atomic concepts (resp. roles) of the signature of K. Additionally, if $(\phi'_1, .., \phi'_n)$ designate the random axioms successively added to K, it was required for each ϕ'_i that $K \cup \{\phi'_1, .., \phi'_i\}$ was consistent, and that there was at least one consequence of the form $A(e)$ or $\neg A(e)$ entailed by $K \cup \{\phi'_1, .., \phi'_i\}$ but not by $K \cup \{\phi'_1, .., \phi'_{i-1}\}$, and such that e shares at least one n-gram with some other named individual of the signature of K. 20 axioms in total were added to K. The corpus consisted of approximately 4500 web pages, retrieved in the same way as for the first dataset. Results are presented in table 2. This time, the values are the number and proportion of randomly generated axioms among the first 5, 10 and 20 discarded ones. Because the numbers of generated and trimmed axioms are identical (20), column "prec./rec." estimates both precision and recall. Precision was high for the first discarded axioms when $\mathrm{sc}(\Gamma \setminus \{\phi\})$ was used to order immediate subbases of Γ. But in both cases, the number of randomly generated axioms among the 20 first discarded ones was not significant.

Conclusion

This article proposes an original approach to identify potentially faulty axioms within a (lightweight) OWL knowledge base, trimming it in order to improve its compliance with some automatically gathered linguistic evidence. A score is defined to evaluate the compliance with the linguistic data of subbases of the input KB, exploiting contexts shared by individuals which, according to a subbase, are instances of the same atomic DL concept. An incremental trimming strategy based on this score is then proposed and evaluated.

[4]http://www.neon-project.org/nw/Ontologies

References

Auer, S., J. Demter, M. Martin, and J. Lehmann (2012). LODStats–an extensible framework for high-performance dataset analytics. In *Knowledge Engineering and Knowledge Management*. Springer.

Baader, F. (2003). *The description logic handbook: theory, implementation, and applications*. Cambridge university press.

Benevides, A., G. Guizzardi, B. Braga, and J. Almeida (2010). Validating modal aspects of OntoUML conceptual models using automatically generated visual world structures. *Journal of Universal Computer Science 16*(20).

Buitelaar, P., P. Cimiano, and B. Magnini (2005). *Ontology Learning from Text: Methods, Evaluation And Applications*. IOS Press.

Cimiano, P. (2006). *Ontology learning and population from text: algorithms, evaluation and applications*. Springer.

Cimiano, P. and J. Völker (2005). Towards large-scale, open-domain and ontology-based named entity classification. In *RANLP proceedings*.

Corman, J., L. Vieu, and N. Aussenac-Gilles (2015). Ontological Analysis For Description Logics Knowledge Base Debugging. In *CommonSense proceedings*.

Ferré, S. and S. Rudolph (2012). Advocatus Diaboli–Exploratory Enrichment of Ontologies with Negative Constraints. *EKAW proceedings*.

Friedrich, G. and K. Shchekotykhin (2005). A general diagnosis method for ontologies. In *ISWC proceedings*.

Giuliano, C. and A. Gliozzo (2008). Instance-based ontology population exploiting named-entity substitution. In *COLING proceedings*.

Hearst, M. A. (1992). Automatic acquisition of hyponyms from large text corpora. In *COLING proceedings*.

Kalyanpur, A., B. Parsia, E. Sirin, and B. Cuenca-Grau (2006). Repairing unsatisfiable concepts in OWL ontologies. In *ESWC proceedings*.

Mendes, P. N., M. Jakob, and C. Bizer (2012). DBpedia: A Multilingual Cross-domain Knowledge Base. In *LREC proceedings*.

Pammer, V. (2010). *Automatic Support for Ontology Evaluation*. Ph. D. thesis, Graz University of Technology.

Poveda-Villalón, M., M. C. Suárez-Figueroa, and A. Gómez-Pérez (2012). Did you validate your ontology? OOPS! In *ESWC proceedings*.

Qi, G., P. Haase, Z. Huang, Q. Ji, J. Z. Pan, and J. Völker (2008). A kernel revision operator for terminologies - algorithms and evaluation. In *ISWC proceedings*.

Ribeiro, M. M. and R. Wassermann (2009). Base revision for ontology debugging. *Journal of Logic and Computation 19*(5).

Schlobach, S. (2005). Diagnosing terminologies. In *AAAI proceedings*.

Tanev, H. and B. Magnini (2008). Weakly supervised approaches for ontology population. In *conference on Ontology Learning and Population proceedings*.

When is Lying the Right Choice? *

Federico Cerutti[†1], Artemis Parvizi[1], Alice Toniolo[1], Dave Braines[2], Geeth R. de Mel[3], Timothy J. Norman[1], Nir Oren[1], Jeff Z. Pan[1], Gavin Pearson[4], Stephen D. Pipes[2] and Paul Sullivan[5]

[1]University of Aberdeen
[2]Emerging Technologies, IBM
[3]T. J. Watson Research Center, IBM
[4]DSTL
[5]INTELPOINT, Inc.

Abstract

Restricting the spread of sensitive information is important in domains ranging from commerce to military operations. In this position paper, we propose research aimed at exploring techniques for privacy enforcement when humans are the recipient of — possibly obfuscated — information. Such obfuscation could be considered to be a *white lie*, and we argue that determining what information to share and whether it should be obfuscated must be done through *controlled query evaluation*, which depends on each agent's risk/benefit evaluation. We concentrate on machine-human interactions, and note that appropriate specific natural language interfaces need to be developed to handle obfuscation. We propose a solution for creating controlled query evaluation mechanisms based on robust approaches for data representation under uncertainty, viz. $\mathcal{S}$DL-Lite, and propose using ITA Controlled English for natural language generation so as to handle subjectivity. We present the general architecture for our approach, with a focus on the relationship between formal ontology, controlled query evaluation, and natural language.

1 Introduction

Information is valuable, and controlling its spread is critical in domains where partially trusted parties interact with each other, especially in cases where information leakage can have serious economic or life-threatening repercussions. Simultaneously however, information must often be exchanged when cooperation is required to achieve a goal. In this paper, we examine how a balance between these two different pulls can be found through the use of *obfuscation* — the replacement of sensitive data with related information, thereby providing an entity with enough knowledge to achieve a goal while preventing sensitive inferences from being made. The problem of information leakage has already been widely studied within the area of autonomous agents. However, while much work has examined machine-machine contexts, the problem becomes more difficult when humans form part of the system. The ability of people to exploit background knowledge to make additional inferences can allow for more sensitive information to be discovered. However, it also provides more scope for misinformation to propagate.

The problem of obfuscating information for humans thus revolves around determining what natural language information to provide to the user in order to have them make desirable inferences, while

*This research was sponsored by US Army Research laboratory and the UK Ministry of Defence and was accomplished under Agreement Number W911NF-06-3-0001. The views and conclusions contained in this document are those of the authors and should not be interpreted as representing the official policies, either expressed or implied, of the US Army Research Laboratory, the U.S. Government, the UK Ministry of Defense, or the UK Government. The US and UK Governments are authorized to reproduce and distribute reprints for Government purposes notwithstanding any copyright notation hereon.

†Corresponding author: f.cerutti@abdn.ac.uk

preventing undesirable inferences from being made. In this paper, we concentrate on deciding how to translate (portions) of an ontology to natural language. Furthermore, we concentrate on the domain of military intelligence analysis, where probabilities, uncertainty and impreciseness are a natural feature. We thus pay additional attention to the issue of how to express, and obfuscate, uncertainty in natural language. We address both of these issues through the use of $\mathcal{S}$DL-Lite — an extension of a tractable subset of description logics which utilises Dempster-Shafer's theory of evidence to encode uncertainties. (Şensoy et al., 2013) — as underlying ontology language. We then make use of ITA Controlled English (ITA-CE) (Mott, 2010) to translate concepts from $\mathcal{S}$DL-Lite into a natural language form. ITA-CE can easily represent Dempster-Shafer's theory of evidence in semi-structured form (Arunkumar et al., 2013), making it a natural candidate to encode concepts from $\mathcal{S}$DL-Lite. Furthermore, Kuhn (2014) has described ITA-CE as a general purpose language, reliable enough for automatic interpretation but with dominant natural elements and medium expressiveness.[1]

In this paper, we make use of provenance analysis as an exemplar domain. Provenance is becoming increasingly important with the growth in sharing and processing of scientific data. The most widely used representation of provenance is through the W3C standard PROV-O ontology,[2] which encodes provenance through a directed acyclic graph where nodes represent entities, activities or agents. Edges are labelled, and encode how nodes interact with each other. Idika et al. (2013) propose a probabilistic extension of traditional provenance graphs and Acar et al. (2013) introduce a core calculus for provenance which can be exploited for privacy enforcement. As discussed below, we seek to identify how information about provenance should be exchanged so as to achieve some (human or artificial) agent's goals, and demonstrate how and why obfuscation might be required.

The remainder of the paper is organised as follows. In Section 2, we present a motivational example, while in Section 3 we discuss the state-of-the-art with regards to approaches for controlled query evaluation and ontological reasoning under uncertainty. We then outline the main questions we will address in this research (Section 4), sketching the theoretical contribution required to make an impact when addressing machine-to-human interaction, our ultimate goal. In Section 5, we conclude the paper by discussing the evaluation procedures we will adopt for ensuring the soundness and correctness of our approach.

2 Motivation

Miles and Ella are two analysts operating as part of an Italy-UK-US coalition. They are tasked with determining the causes of an unidentified illness affecting livestock in an area under coalition control. They have been provided with a report indicating engineered non-waterborne contamination in the local water system. This report originated from an analysis by a UK based lab. However, this analysis was — to the best of the analysts' knowledge — performed by a third-party (non-governmental organisation) chemist. Additional uncertainties in the report arise as it could be the case that the chemist utilised data from what was assumed to be a water sample, which was expected to be generated by the sampling activity of what was claimed to be an Italian Water Sensor. This provenance chain is depicted in Figure 1 via the solid black lines.

Now assume that Miles works for the UK army and has access to the data presented above, while Ella is an analyst who is working for the US army. Miles shares only the final result with Ella the information "the water is contaminated", avoiding the sharing of provenance information.[3] However Ella can ask Miles specific questions regarding provenance, such as "who are the actors involved in this analysis?" (**Q1**). The answer can be "the involved actors are Italian sensors (likely), NGO chemist (possibly), and UK lab (almost certain)." Choosing the best term among *possibly*, *certain*, ..., can affect further inferences by Ella, and is one of the main problems we want to address.

[1]Classification $P^3E^3N^3S^3$ — reliably interpretable languages (P^3) with medium expressiveness (E^3); dominant natural elements (N^3); and lengthy descriptions (S^3) (Kuhn, 2014, Table 2).

[2]`http://www.w3.org/TR/prov-o/`.

[3]See `http://www.smh.com.au/articles/2003/07/02/1056825430340.html` for a real world example.

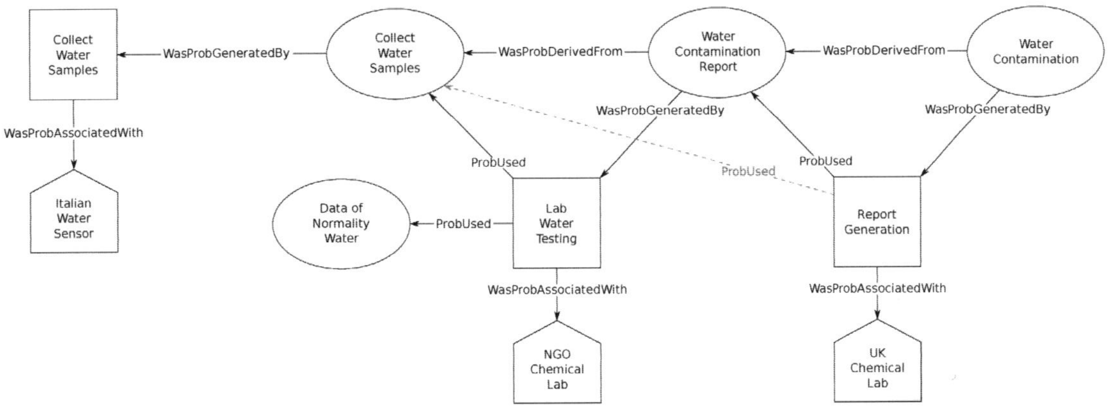

Figure 1: Provenance associated with the statement "the water is contaminated". The dashed red line encodes the added relation (aimed at maintaining consistency with the white lie) "the UK did not use only the results coming from the NGO chemist." Round nodes represent Entities, Squares represent Activities, and Pentagonal shapes represent Agents.

Moreover, Ella can in turn ask "did the UK lab use only the results coming from the NGO chemist?" (**Q2**). Miles knows that the results provided by the NGO are reliable, but Ella does not. Moreover, Ella might consider "collateral knowledge" or biases (e.g., "by default every NGO is unreliable"), and thus a positive answer would result in a loss of trust. Miles therefore has two choices for a response:

- abstain from providing the information: e.g. "I cannot tell you this"; or
- tell a white lie: e.g. "the UK did not only use the results coming from the NGO chemist."

Identifying the best strategy is difficult; abstaining from answering can lead Ella to derive what should be kept confidential (Sicherman et al., 1983). At the same time, obfuscating information is a complex activity as Miles must maintain consistency during his interaction with Ella. For instance, since Miles already shared the information "The NGO chemist is possibly involved in the analysis," he cannot retract this information. Therefore, one approach to maintaining consistency is to change the provenance graph by showing that the UK final report has been generated both from the NGO analysis and from the original water sample, as indicated by the red dashed arrow in Figure 1.

3 Background

3.1 Controlled Query Evaluation

Controlled Query Evaluation (CQE) is a framework for confidentiality enforcement, first proposed by Sicherman et al. (1983), and then developed in several other works, e.g. (Cuenca Grau et al., 2013; Biskup et al., 2014). We describe the main elements for a CQE framework based on the approach proposed by Biskup et al. (2014).

First of all, a *world view* is presented as a sequence $\langle \Gamma; \varphi_1, \ldots, \varphi_n \rangle$, where $\varphi_i \in \mathcal{L}$ are observations from a language $\mathcal{L}$, and Γ is the *background knowledge* (e.g., collateral knowledge, or even biases) over a language $\mathcal{L}_\Gamma$, which extends $\mathcal{L}$ to express rules.

Agents can form *beliefs* about $\varphi \in \mathcal{L}$ using the Bel operators, which belongs to a family of operators Ξ, such that $Bel : 2^{\mathcal{L}_\Gamma} \times \mathcal{L}^* \mapsto 2^{\mathcal{L}}$. We say that the agent believes φ using Bel if $\varphi \in Bel(\langle \Gamma; \varphi_1, \ldots, \varphi_n \rangle)$.

Each belief operator $Bel \in \Xi$ satisfies:

- *consistency* — $\nexists \varphi \in \mathcal{L}, W \in 2^{\mathcal{L}_\Gamma} \times \mathcal{L}^*$ s.t. $\varphi \in Bel(W)$ and $\neg\varphi \in Bel(W)$;
- *propositional consequence* — $\forall \varphi, \psi \in \mathcal{L}$, if $\varphi \vdash \psi$, $\forall W \in 2^{\mathcal{L}_\Gamma} \times \mathcal{L}^*$, $\varphi \in Bel(W)$ implies $\psi \in Bel(W)$.

Moreover $\preceq_{cred}$ is an ordering over Ξ such that if $Bel \preceq_{cred} Bel'$ (Bel' is at least as credulous as Bel), then $\forall W \in 2^{\mathcal{L}_\Gamma} \times \mathcal{L}^*$, $Bel(W) \subseteq Bel'(W)$.

In particular, let $\Xi^{RW} = \{Bel_p \mid p \in (0.5, 1]\}$, where $Bel_p(\langle \Gamma; \varphi_1, \ldots, \varphi_n \rangle) = \{\varphi \in \mathcal{L} \mid \delta(\varphi, \langle \Gamma; \varphi_1, \ldots, \varphi_n \rangle \geq p)\}$, with $\delta(\varphi, \langle \Gamma; \varphi_1, \ldots, \varphi_n \rangle) = \frac{|\mu(\varphi) \cap \mu(\Gamma \cup \{\varphi_1, \ldots, \varphi_n\})|}{|\mu(\Gamma \cup \{\varphi_1, \ldots, \varphi_n\})|}$, assuming that $\Gamma \cup \{\varphi_1, \ldots, \varphi_n\}$ is consistent and $\mu(\cdot)$ is a model operator (Bacchus, 1996). $Bel_p \preceq^{RW}_{cred} Bel_{p'}$ iff $p' \leq p$.

When an agent becomes aware that sentence $\varphi \in \mathcal{L}$ holds, i.e., when $\tau(\varphi) = \top$ with $\tau(\cdot)$ denoting a truth function, as the result of the speech act $inform(\varphi) \in Act$, it appends φ to its observation using the operator $+ : 2^{\mathcal{L}_\Gamma} \times \mathcal{L}^* \times Act \mapsto 2^{\mathcal{L}_\Gamma} \times \mathcal{L}^*$ s.t. $\langle \Gamma; \varphi_1, \ldots, \varphi_n \rangle + inform(\varphi) = \langle \Gamma; \varphi_1, \ldots, \varphi_n, \varphi \rangle$.

A secrecy policy is then a set of secrecy constraints such that each constraint is of the form $\langle \varphi, Bel \rangle \in \mathcal{L} \times \Xi$ which expresses the desire to avoid that an agent believes φ when using the operator Bel.

In sharing a sentence, each agent must make assumptions about the recipient's world view and its choice of Bel operator for that sentence. This is encoded via a non-empty set of world views denoted the *postulated world view*.

Biskup et al. (2014) provides principles for a secrecy reasoner by taking into consideration a set of postulated world views and a set of possible actions to be classified:

- I.1: (*avoid potential violations*) it is desirable to avoid that in some of the postulated world views more secrecy constraints become violated;
- I.2: (*mitigate potential violations*) if a sentence cannot be protected against inferences with Bel as desired, it should at least be protected against inferences with operators less credulous than Bel;
- II: (*minimise classification*) a classification should be as minimally restrictive as possible w.r.t. other desires such as cooperative information sharing;
- III: (*be cautious towards credulous reasoners*) the more credulous the belief operator is postulated to be in a secrecy constraint, the more cautious an agent has to be while acting;
- IV: (*be more cautious the more uncertain*) the more world views a recipient holds according to the postulated world views, the more uncertain the situation is.

Moreover, a generic algorithm for implementing a secrecy reasoner is also provided in (Biskup et al., 2014, § 4) which we do not review here due to space constraints. It is worth noticing that Biskup et al. (2014)'s approach is propositional: each sentence φ is either true ($\tau(\varphi) = \top$) or false ($\tau(\varphi) = \bot$) and $inform(\varphi)$ implies that the recipient knows that φ holds ($\tau(\varphi) = \top$). For our scenario, discussed in Section 2, this is not enough as we need to consider uncertainties and probabilities.

3.2 Subjective DL-lite

Şensoy et al. (2013) introduce the $\mathcal{S}$DL-Lite formalism, which is an extension of a tractable subset of Description Logics with Dempster-Shafer Theory (DST) of evidence. In DST, a *binomial opinion* — or *SL opinion* — about a proposition ϕ is represented by a triple $w_\phi = \langle b(\phi), d(\phi), u(\phi) \rangle$, where $b(\phi)$ is the belief about ϕ — the summation of the probability masses that entail ϕ; $d(\phi)$ is the disbelief about ϕ — the summation of the probability masses that entail $\neg\phi$; $u(\phi)$ is the uncertainty about ϕ — the summation of the probability masses that entail neither ϕ nor $\neg\phi$; and $b(\phi) + d(\phi) + u(\phi) = 1$.

A DL-lite knowledge base $\mathcal{K} = \langle \mathcal{T}, \mathcal{A} \rangle$ consists of a TBox $\mathcal{T}$ and an ABox $\mathcal{A}$. Axioms are either

- class inclusion axioms: $B \sqsubseteq C \in \mathcal{T}$ where B is a basic class $B := \mathsf{A} \mid \exists R \mid \exists R^-$ (A denotes a named class, R a named property, and R^- the inverse of R) and C is a general class $C := B \mid \neg B \mid C_1 \sqcap C_2$; or
- individual axioms: $B(\mathsf{a}), R(\mathsf{a}, \mathsf{b}) \in \mathcal{A}$ where a and b are named individuals.

$\mathcal{S}$DL-Lite (Şensoy et al., 2013) is an extension of DL-lite with subjective opinion assertions of the form $\mathcal{B} : w$ where w is an opinion and $\mathcal{B}$ is an ABox axiom. Let $\mathcal{W}$ be the set of all possible subjective binary opinions. A subjective interpretation is a pair $\mathcal{I} = \langle \Delta^\mathcal{I}, \cdot^\mathcal{I} \rangle$, where the domain $\Delta^\mathcal{I}$ is a non-empty set of objects, and $\cdot^\mathcal{I}$ is a subjective interpretation function, which maps:

- an individual a to an element of $\mathsf{a}^\mathcal{I} \in \Delta^\mathcal{I}$;

- a named class A to a function $A^{\mathcal{I}} : \Delta^{\mathcal{I}} \mapsto \mathcal{W}$;
- a named property R to a function $R^{\mathcal{I}} : \Delta^{\mathcal{I}} \times \Delta^{\mathcal{I}} \mapsto \mathcal{W}$.

The complete specification of the semantics of $\mathcal{S}$DL-Lite is given in Table 1.

Syntax	Semantics
$\top$	$\top^{\mathcal{I}}(o) = \langle 1,0,0 \rangle$
$\bot$	$\bot^{\mathcal{I}}(o) = \langle 0,1,0 \rangle$
$\exists R$	$b((\exists R)^{\mathcal{I}}(o_1)) \geq \max \bigcup_{\forall o_2} \{b(R^{\mathcal{I}}(o_1,o_2))\}$ and $d((\exists R)^{\mathcal{I}}(o_1)) \leq \min \bigcup_{\forall o_2} \{d(R^{\mathcal{I}}(o_1,o_2))\}$
$\neg B$	$(\neg B)^{\mathcal{I}}(o) = \neg B^{\mathcal{I}}(o)$
R^-	$(R^-)^{\mathcal{I}}(o_2,o_1) = R^{\mathcal{I}}(o_1,o_2)$

Syntax	Semantics
$B_1 \sqsubseteq B_2$	$\forall o \in \Delta^{\mathcal{I}}, b(B_1{}^{\mathcal{I}}(o)) \leq b(B_2{}^{\mathcal{I}}(o))$ and $d(B_2{}^{\mathcal{I}}(o)) \leq d(B_1{}^{\mathcal{I}}(o))$
$B_1 \sqsubseteq \neg B_2$	$\forall o \in \Delta^{\mathcal{I}}, b(B_1{}^{\mathcal{I}}(o)) \leq d(B_2{}^{\mathcal{I}}(o))$ and $b(B_2{}^{\mathcal{I}}(o)) \leq d(B_1{}^{\mathcal{I}}(o))$
$B(\mathsf{a}) : w$	$b(w) \leq b(B^{\mathcal{I}}(\mathsf{a}^{\mathcal{I}}))$ and $d(w) \leq d(B^{\mathcal{I}}(\mathsf{a}^{\mathcal{I}}))$
$R(\mathsf{a},\mathsf{b}) : w$	$b(w) \leq b(R^{\mathcal{I}}(\mathsf{a}^{\mathcal{I}},\mathsf{b}^{\mathcal{I}}))$ and $d(w) \leq d(R^{\mathcal{I}}(\mathsf{a}^{\mathcal{I}},\mathsf{b}^{\mathcal{I}}))$

Table 1: Semantics of $\mathcal{S}$DL-Lite.

4 CQE Procedures for Provenance and ITA-CE Interfaces

The ultimate goal of this research is to provide computationally effective strategies for controlled query evaluation over uncertain knowledge bases with (controlled) natural language interfaces, thereby allowing the information recipient to be a human user. In particular, we focus on provenance due to its importance in domains such as intelligence analysis, and because it has a constrained domain ontology. Previous works, e.g. (Acar et al., 2013), examine privacy enforcement techniques for provenance, which provide a useful baseline for comparison.

There are three main concepts in the ontology presented in Figure 1, namely E (Entity), Ac (Activity), and Ag (Agent); and a variety of properties, such as R_{Assoc} (WasProbAssociatedWith), R_{Gen} (WasProbGeneratedBy), R_U (ProbUsed), R_{Der} (WasProbDerivedFrom). Thus, the answer to the first query (**Q1**) of Section 2 — "the involved actors are Italian sensors (*likely*),..." — could be the result of the following fragment in the knowledge base:

- $Ag(\mathsf{itwatsensor}) : \langle 1,0,0 \rangle$ (it is "certain" that "Italian Water Sensor" is an Agent);
- $Ac(\mathsf{collectwater}) : \langle 1,0,0 \rangle$ (it is "certain" that "Collect Water Samples" is an Action);
- $R_{Assoc}(\mathsf{collectwater}, \mathsf{itwatsensor}) : \langle 0.7, 0.01, 0.29 \rangle$ (it is "*likely*" that the Italian sensor is related to the water sampling activity).

The relationship between the concept *likely*, defined as "Such as well might happen or be true; probable," and the opinion $\langle 0.7, 0.01, 0.29 \rangle$, which could be encoded as "being certain at 70%, and admitting ignorance for 29% of cases," is clearly far from being universally acceptable. One of the difficulties of dealing with uncertain knowledge bases and humans, and also one of our main research questions, is *which are the suitable fuzzy categories for representing uncertainty in a machine-to-human dialogue*?

Moreover, in order to deal with subjective logic opinions, we extend the CQE framework by considering $\mathcal{S}$DL-Lite knowledge bases. Given a $\mathcal{S}$DL-Lite knowledge base $\mathcal{K}$, a sentence φ has an SL opinion associated to it — i.e., $\tau(\varphi) = w \in \mathcal{W}$. We can identify some limit-cases w.r.t. the propositional approach described in Section 3, namely $\top = \langle 1,0,0 \rangle$ and $\bot = \langle 0,1,0 \rangle$. Furthermore, as we already consider SL opinions associated to sentences, we will also extend the definition of Ξ^{RW} to $\Xi^{SL} = \{Bel_w \mid w \in \mathcal{W}\}$ thus applying opportune thresholds.

In addition, as a human engages in a querying process which might involve a white lie, coherence among the information shared during the dialogue must be ensured. This can be partially addressed by using belief revision approaches (Gärdenfors, 2005) in conjunction with plausibility metrics (Ma and Liu, 2008). This highlights another interesting question — similar to the one investigated by Cerutti et al. (2014) — viz. *are theoretically sound plausibility metrics useful in interacting with human users*?

Finally, formal results regarding privacy enforcement in the context of provenance, might be reused here (Acar et al., 2013). These approaches adopt very general languages to represent provenance traces but do not consider uncertainty. A way to abstract our representation of provenance data, to be able to reuse some of the results of Acar et al. (2013), is (1) to identify the actions in a provenance graph; (2) to create clusters around the action nodes; (3) to analyse the resulting clustered graph — potentially via a (probabilistic) finite automaton — as a probabilistic Kripke structure and represent it using probabilistic computational tree logic (CTL) (Kleinberg, 2012, Chapter 3). In this way, we could easily provide an answer to query (**Q2**), viz. "did the UK lab use only the results coming from the NGO chemist?" This thus raises the following question: *how to support a human user in querying provenance data*?

In our proposed use of ITA-CE as the Controlled Natural Language representation we also recognize that a well-known trait of Controlled Languages and Controlled Vocabularies is that they are "easy to read, hard to write" (Preece et al., 2014; Braines et al., 2014). Traditional solutions involved training and tooling to assist the user in constructing valid and meaningful sentences in these languages. In the work proposed here we envisage a system that provides maximum utility to untrained users in situations where they may have very limited support from tooling or custom applications. Example usage could include an SMS text message interface, or a Siri-like spoken conversation interaction. Therefore in related research (Preece et al., 2014; Braines et al., 2014) we are investigating human-machine conversational interaction where the human agent is able to express their input (assertion, question etc) in Natural Language, with the system providing an answer or interpretation in ITA-CE, thereby mitigating the "hard to write" aspect by enabling the user to provide Natural Language input, and confirming the machine interpretation by showing the human user the ITA-CE interpretation which we assert is "easy to read."

From a technical perspective, Ibbotson et al. (2012) develop a representation of the PROV-O using ITA-CE, and discuss how this can provide a narrative of the provenance documentation. While the model is fully integrated, the query procedure is still quite preliminary. Instead, Ibbotson et al. (2012) focus more on the relationship with trust and exploit one of the capabilities of ITA-CE, namely its ability to *explain* query results through chains of "because" statement (*rationale*). However, Ibbotson et al. (2012) do not consider neither uncertain knowledge, nor the need for privacy.

5 Conclusion

In this paper we outline the main elements for a research program aimed at ensuring privacy enforcement in shared information when humans are in the loop. As a case-study we consider the provenance record associated with information. Some approaches for privacy enforcement of provenance have recently been proposed although they focus on representation models quite distant from ontology-based ones, which are those of interest for us. Indeed, we want to develop an approach as general as possible — exploiting results related to controlled query evaluation approaches — thus relying on general ways to represent domain knowledge. To this end we chose to adopt an advanced description logic, namely $\mathcal{S}$DL-Lite, which is built on top of DL-lite, extending it with Dempster-Shafer's theory of evidence.

This brings us to one of the main components of our architecture, namely the choice of the ITA Controlled English ITA-CE (Mott, 2010). ITA-CE has the unique capability to handle subjective logic opinions (Arunkumar et al., 2013), and it has been shown to be able to encompass the PROV-O model of provenance (Ibbotson et al., 2012) with some basic query process. Our goal is to develop a natural language interface for our CQE approach. This is a key element as we plan to adopt it for evaluating this work through experiments involving human users, which, hopefully, will in turn guide the development of the underlying theory. Theoretical properties of intermediate results will be also evaluated either in connection with the relevant literature or comparing them against clear and intuitive desiderata.

Finally, additional interesting elements will be investigated, in particular the connection between time and privacy. There are naturally situations where the need of privacy is strictly related to time. For instance, to successfully rescue hostages, their position must be kept secret until the rescue operation is concluded (Cerutti et al., 2014). After the hostages are safe, there is no longer a need for keeping such a secret. Moreover, time and trust are strictly related as "distrust may be expected to retard the rate of information dissemination through a network" (Huynh et al., 2010). Similarly, a time-varying sharing effort can affect the trust perceived by the other members of a coalition.

References

Acar, U. A., A. Ahmed, J. Cheney, and R. Perera (2013). A core calculus for provenance. *J. of Comp. Sec. 21*(6), 919–969.

Arunkumar, S., M. Srivatsa, D. Braines, and M. Sensoy (2013). Assessing trust over uncertain rules and streaming data. In *FUSION*, pp. 1–8.

Bacchus, F. (1996). From statistical knowledge bases to degrees of belief. *Artif. Intell. 87*(1-2), 75–143.

Biskup, J., G. Kern-Isberner, P. Krümpelmann, and C. Tadros (2014). Reasoning on Secrecy Constraints under Uncertainty to Classify Possible Actions. In *FoIKS 2014*, pp. 97–116.

Braines, D., A. Preece, G. de Mel, and T. Pham (2014). Enabling CoIST users: D2D at the network edge. In *FUSION*, pp. 1–8.

Cerutti, F., G. R. de Mel, T. J. Norman, N. Oren, A. Parvizi, P. Sullivan, and A. Toniolo (2014). Obfuscation of Semantic Data: Restricting the Spread of Sensitive Information. In *DL2014*.

Cerutti, F., N. Tintarev, and N. Oren (2014). Formal Arguments, Preferences, and Natural Language Interfaces to Humans: an Empirical Evaluation. In *ECAI*, pp. 207–212.

Şensoy, M., A. Fokoue, J. Z. Pan, T. J. Norman, Y. Tang, N. Oren, and K. Sycara (2013). Reasoning about uncertain information and conflict resolution through trust revision. In *AAMAS*, pp. 837–844.

Cuenca Grau, B., E. Kharlamov, E. V. Kostylev, and D. Zheleznyakov (2013). Controlled Query Evaluation over OWL 2 RL Ontologies. In *ISWC*, pp. 49–65.

Gärdenfors, P. (2005). *The Dynamics of Thought*, Volume 300 of *Synthese Library*. Springer Netherlands.

Huynh, T. D., P. R. Smart, D. Braines, N. Shadbolt, and K. Sycara (2010). The Cognitive Virtues of Dynamic Networks. In *ACITA'10*.

Ibbotson, J., D. Braines, D. Mott, S. Arunkumar, and M. Srivatsa (2012). Documenting Provenance with a Controlled Natural Language. `https://www.usukita.org/node/2186`.

Idika, N., M. Varia, and H. Phan (2013). The Probabilistic Provenance Graph. In *SPW*, pp. 34–41.

Kleinberg, S. (2012). *Causality, Probability, and Time*. Cambridge University Press.

Kuhn, T. (2014). A Survey and Classification of Controlled Natural Languages. *Comp. Ling. 40*(1), 121–170.

Ma, J. and W. Liu (2008). A General Model for Epistemic State Revision using Plausibility Measures. In *ECAI*, pp. 356–360.

Mott, D. (2010). Summary of ITA controlled English. Technical report.

Preece, A., D. Braines, D. Pizzocaro, and C. Parizas (2014). Human-machine conversations to support multi-agency missions. *MC2R 18*(1), 75–84.

Sicherman, G. L., W. De Jonge, and R. P. Van de Riet (1983). Answering queries without revealing secrets. *ACM Trans. on Database Syst. 8*(1), 41–59.

AUTHOR INDEX